Praise for "Stronghold"...

"Karen's message is a powerful one; a message of survival through faith. Karen takes you on a journey through her painful past, and how God's unfailing love stayed with her and ultimately led her to a fulfilling life of love. Her real experiences with domestic violence makes the statistics more personal, and gives the reader an inside look into the pain suffered by victims of domestic violence. Not only is she a brave woman to have survived what she did, but now she also shares her story to help others, a testimony of her faith and perseverance."

    Cathi Brese Doebler, author of "Ditch the Joneses, Discover Your Family: How to Thrive on Less Than Two Incomes!"

"Overall, Stronghold was a great book to read. As someone fairly new to the field of domestic violence, I found the facts about DV very helpful, especially as Karen related them to her own personal experiences. By providing facts and her story, she really conveyed the message of how domestic violence affects people daily and the struggles someone could face. I think that this is a great resource for anyone to learn from. I hope that the book continues to educate those who know nothing about domestic violence as well as inspire those in similar situations through Karen's strength and courage. Thank you, Karen, for sharing your story and educating others about the effects of domestic violence."
    Emily W. , Haven House

"As an educator and Clinical Psychologist over the past 28 years, I have come to know the profound sadness and brokenness of children, adolescents, women and families that have experienced the trauma of physical, emotional and sexual abuse. The depth of their grief,

disillusionment, and sense of hopelessness is unfathomable. As a vessel and conduit of God working with these individuals, I have also seen and have been able to experience the joy in their healing, their new sense of self, and their ability to forgive. I want to thank Karen for allowing me to read her story "Stronghold" and experience her tumultuous journey and ever present relationship with God. Domestic violence is much too rampant and under acknowledged in this world that we live in. It is with these stories written by strong, independent, self-empowered and God-loving women like Karen that will bring a spotlight to this issue and become a safety net for others who are currently experiencing the effects of domestic violence. Again, thank you Karen, for sharing your story. I am most humbled!"

  Dr. Debra L. Martinez, Clinical Psychologist

"Once I started reading, I couldn't stop! A very compelling story. Thank you, Karen, for an unfiltered look inside the life of a victim of domestic abuse. Your story is a powerful example of cashing in on God's promise to turn brokenness into perfect purpose."

  Valerie S.

"'Stronghold' is a captivating and insightful memoir of childhood sexual assault leading into horrendous domestic violence experiences and survivorship - all navigated through the power of Christian spirituality. Poignant narratives are intermingled with pertinent information on psychological patterns, up-to-date facts and statistics, and pragmatic guidance for victims to escape from the cycle of violence. Anyone suffering from the shame and isolation of abuse will want to read this transformative success story."

  Pamela M. Hughes, Counseling Psychologist, Licensed Clinical Social Worker

STRONGHOLD

One Woman's Journey of
Survival and Healing
from Domestic Violence

Karen D'Ingillo

STRONGHOLD

by Karen D'Ingillo

© 2015

All rights reserved. No portion of this book may be reproduced, stored in a retrieval system, or transmitted in any form or by any means—electronic, mechanical, photocopy, recording, scanning, or other—except for brief quotations in critical reviews or articles, without the prior written permission of the publisher.

Published in Los Angeles, California by Little Red Wagon Publishing.

All Scripture quotations are taken from the Holy Bible, New International Version, unless otherwise indicated. Used by permission from Zondervan Corporation.

Cover artwork from Jonathan Rogers, Niagara Falls, New York. Used by Permission.

Cover design from Leslie Sears, LES is MORE Printing and Graphics, Kurtistown, Hawaii.

Names in this book have been changed or omitted to protect the identities of the persons involved.Library of Congress Copyright Registration Number #

ISBN 978-0692482667

Library of Congress Control Number #

Library of Congress Cataloging-in-Publication Data

D'Ingillo, Karen

    Stronghold: One Woman's Journey of Survival and Healing from Domestic Violence/Karen D'Ingillo

Includes bibliographical references and index

ISBN 978-0692482667

1. Abuse 2. Christianity - Christian Living

Printed in the United States of America

This book is dedicated to each and every person who has been touched by and had their lives changed because of domestic violence.

May you be granted the strength and perseverance to push forward to a better life and assist in the fight to end this senseless crime.

"Never, never be afraid to do what's right, especially if the well-being of a person or animal is at stake. Society's punishments are small compared to the wounds we inflict on our soul when we look the other way."

"Justice will not be served until those who are unaffected are as outraged as those who are."

Thank you from the bottom of my heart to everyone who has been there for me...
to assist and encourage me through the difficult times and rejoice with me in the happiest of times.

Your support has meant more to me than words can express.

Acknowledgments

The seed of this book began as a speech. As time passed, many people who were dealing with domestic violence crossed my path. As I listened to their stories, I became more passionate about sharing mine. I have received tremendous support from friends and family as I have moved forward with this project that I have held so near and dear to my heart.

Jim...I love you. I have been blessed beyond measure to have you as my husband. I appreciate your wisdom and insight, and your abounding love and support. I appreciate all that you bring into my life, especially the laughter. I am a better person because you are in my life.

My children...my greatest blessings that have brought me such endless joy. I love each of you from the depths of my heart.

My sister and brother...you have always been there for me, in spite of geographical distances...praying and chanting. Your support means so very much. I love you.

My lifelong best friend S.B....I cannot ever imagine life without you in it. I love you so much. You have travelled this historic road with me. You have supported me, loved me, and survived with me. I am deeply grateful for your lifelong friendship.

My friends...deepest thanks for your support. You each know who you are. Some of you are on the east coast, and some of you are on the west coast, and there are too many of you to mention by name. Your support and encouragement has meant so much.

Cathi, Deb, Val, Pam, and Emily...your kind words of support. Thank you so much.

Special thanks to Jonathan Rogers...for the beautiful artistry that you share with the world and for allowing the blessing of your artwork as the cover of my book.

My high school English teacher...who encouraged me from tenth grade to keep writing. My college writing professor...who wrote in my college yearbook, "You'll always be my best writer. You better keep at it so someday I can pick up a magazine or book written by Karen." My other college writing professor, who in 2008, inspired me to reach into the depths of myself to be the very best writer I could be. My thanks to each of you for your words of encouragement. This book is a product of that encouragement and inspiration.

Table of Contents

Introduction

Chapter One: "Jane"

Chapter Two: "Welcome to My World"

Chapter Three: "What is Domestic Violence?"

Chapter Four: "Betrayal"

Chapter Five: "The Dating Game"

Chapter Six: "Love Hurts"

Chapter Seven: "Why Stay?"

Chapter Eight: "How to Help"

Chapter Nine: "Public Awareness"

Chapter Ten: "A Safety Plan"

Chapter Eleven: "Facing Goliath"

Chapter Twelve: "Moving Forward"

Chapter Thirteen: "Secret Places of My Heart"

Chapter Fourteen: "Discovery"

Chapter Fifteen: "Forgiveness"

Epilogue

Appendix

Introduction

The current statistics concerning domestic violence make me want to cry and scream all at the same time. The numbers are heartbreaking. According to the National Coalition Against Domestic Violence (NCADV), here are the current statistics:

- One in every four women will be affected by domestic violence in her lifetime.

- 85% of domestic violence victims are women.

- One in twelve women will be stalked by a current or former intimate partner.

- 81% of these women stalked will also be physically assaulted.

- Almost 1/3 of female homicides were committed by an intimate partner.

- Only ¼ of all assaults against women by intimate partners are reported.

- 1.3 million women each year are affected by intimate partner violence.

- The cost of intimate partner violence exceeds $5.8 billion each year - $4.1 billion is for direct medical and mental health services.

- There are 16,800 homicides and $2.2 million in medically treated injuries due to intimate partner violence."[1]

We live in a violent world. This hideous problem of domestic violence is growing to epidemic proportions. Reading the stories and statistics may make you angry. They may make you want to do something about it. They may make you say, "This is not my problem." With a one in four statistic, the chances are pretty good that you know a woman who is being abused, who has been abused or will be abused.

I was one of those women. I was one of those statistics. Thankfully, I am one of those statistics on the survivor side of the story, not on the homicide side of the story. Throughout my experiences, I met people who wanted to help, who wanted to make a difference for me. There were people who wanted to share meals with me and show me how to do things that I did not know how to do. There were people who wanted to be resources to point me in

---

[1] National Coalition Against Domestic Violence: www.cadv.org

the right direction. I also met people who told me that it was not their problem and they turned the other way. "You must have deserved it," they would say. I did not deserve the bruises, the broken bones, or the black eyes. I did not deserve to have my husband whisper "sweet nothings" in my ear, except the "sweet nothings" he referred to were that I would taste nothing but death that night when I closed my eyes to sleep. "Death will be sweet." he would say. I did not deserve to be treated the way I was treated. I did not deserve to feel so alone and isolated, imprisoned, beaten, forsaken and unworthy of anything good. I deserved so much better than that. I was made for so much more.

The journey through this life is not always what we hope for or dream of. Our plans may become derailed and the clarity of our vision may become obscured. Sometimes the darkness of our storms surrounds us and takes away our hope. There may be times when we don't know where to turn, who to trust, or what step to take next. Storms are a certainty of life. There are lessons to be learned from these storms. Go through the storm. Don't try to detour around it to avoid the darkness. Endure it. The storm is developing your character, teaching you lessons and making you stronger. Storms can be frightening, especially when you feel you've lost your way. Remember, this too shall pass. The storm will eventually end and you will be changed because of it. You will be a better version of yourself on the other side of it.

A stronghold is defined as "a fortified place or fortress; a place of survival or refuge."[3] A stronghold is also "Satan's power."[4] In my life's journey, Satan has used the stronghold of abuse to keep me locked in a state of paralyzing fear, unable to move forward. All I could feel was guilt, shame, anger, pain, embarrassment, hopelessness and a complete lack of self-esteem. I was a nobody. I was in the midst of a very dark storm. On the other side of that storm, I realized that God held me in the palms of His hands. God had planned so much more for my life than the abuse I had suffered. He may have allowed things to happen to me, but He never abandoned me. He had a purpose and a plan for each of those things. In the safety of His hands, God became my stronghold, my place of survival and refuge. God protected me. As I share my story, you will clearly see God's hand in my life. When the storms surrounded me with darkness, His light made the way for me. He helped me face my paralyzing fear and break free from the strongholds that were weighing me down.

---

3 www.thefreedictionary.com

4 Life Application NIV Study Bible (Wheaton, Illinois and Grand Rapids, Michigan: Tyndale House Publishers and Zondervan Corporation, 2005), 2367.

I believe that the Bible is God's Word, spoken as promises and instruction to His people over 2000 years ago. The instructions and promises within the pages of this book hold just as true today as the day they were written. God is constant. He does not change. God promises that He will lead us and guide us, that He is close to the brokenhearted, and that He has a plan for each of our lives. Our lives have purpose. Our lives have a chosen destiny. God is able to take everything that happens to us and use it for our good. Sometimes that is hard to see and understand. I am so grateful that God can take the brokenness of our lives and put the pieces back together. I am so grateful that He has more planned for my life than the abuse I have endured and survived. Mostly, I am grateful that, no matter what, He keeps me safe in the palms of His hands.

If you are in the midst of a dark storm right now, and you are being broken by domestic violence, be encouraged. You are not alone. Others have gone before you and survived. Others are behind you, following in your footsteps, hoping you will show them the way to go. There is life beyond domestic violence, abuse and trauma. God is with you every step of the way, whether you acknowledge Him or not, because He has big plans for you. Let Him be your stronghold. He will not let you down.

Chapter One

"Jane"

Sharing my story of survival actually began as a college assignment. This was not college that enters your life on the heels of graduating from high school. This was returning to college at the young age of 50 years old to earn a new degree. The Presentational Speaking class was the last place I thought I would find myself. I took a deep breath as I stepped up to the podium and began my speech.

"What do you associate with the following items: a baseball bat, a deck of cards, money, tears, a knife, strawberries, lighter fluid, a gun, and laughter? For one woman, these are all associations to the abuse she suffered at the hands of her husband in her own home. This, by a man who promised to love and cherish her, in a place that should have been her sanctuary.

According to the U.S. Department of Justice, one in every four women will experience domestic violence in their lifetime. Incidents of domestic violence could be decreased through raising public awareness, re-examining and changing attitudes, and eliminating the social tolerance that perpetuates it.

Tonight, we are going to look at this silent killer that plagues our society. I will explain the various forms that domestic violence takes. I will paint a clear picture of a victim. I will explain how easily it is tolerated by society. I will suggest simple ways that you can make a difference by becoming involved.

Domestic violence is physical, emotional, psychological, and/or sexual abuse that occurs within the context of the family home. All racial, social, economic, religious, and ethnic groups are affected. Domestic violence is about power and control. Because the abuser can use various methods to gain power and control, victims live in constant fear.

According to the New York State Office for the Prevention of Domestic Violence, there are nine forms of power and control that are involved in domestic violence. As I explain these nine forms to you, I will also tell you the story of Jane.

- **Intimidation**: Jane's husband made her afraid by using looks, actions, and gestures. He also used weapons against her, such as a baseball bat, a knife, and a gun.

- **Emotional abuse**: He called Jane names and humiliated her.

- **Isolation**: He took away her car, her license, the telephone, stopped the mail and the newspaper to isolate her contact with the outside world.

- **Denying and Blaming**: Jane's husband would deny that he abused her and he would tell her that she caused it or made him do it.

- **Using Children**: He threatened to take her two children away from her. He also used them to obtain information: "What did Mommy do today while Daddy was at work?"

- **Using Male Privilege**: Jane's husband treated her like a servant and defined her role in the household.

- **Economic Abuse**: He made her play cards with him or strip tease for him to earn money for groceries and diapers.

- **Coercion and Threats**: He made threats to hurt or kill her, like saying, "Taste those strawberries now. All you will taste tonight is death."

- **Sexual Abuse**: Jane repeatedly suffered marital rape at knifepoint.

On Jane's last day in her house, her husband poured lighter fluid on her and tried to set her on fire. She and her two children escaped with the help of four police officers. Jane never found out who called 911 to save her.

This is <u>*one woman's*</u> experience. The National Coalition Against Domestic Violence says there are an estimated 1.3 *million* women who are victims of domestic violence each year. This could be someone you know: a neighbor, a roommate, your best friend, your sister, or even your mother. Sadly, only one quarter of these domestic violence crimes are reported, according to the National Coalition.

From a medical standpoint, the Center for Disease Control and Prevention states the costs of domestic violence exceed $5.8 *billion* each year. Of that amount, nearly $4.1 billion are for direct medical and mental health care services and nearly $1.8 billion are for indirect costs of lost productivity and wages.

Today's society has become de-sensitized to the violence around us. There is a social tolerance when it comes to domestic violence. Many people think it is "none of their business". The abuser may say, "I lost my temper", or "I got drunk and out of control", or "I had a bad day at work". These excuses are often accepted without question. The underlying beliefs and attitudes the man holds towards women are more of a factor in domestic violence than their excuses. Generally, the abusers believe they have a right to enforce their will on their female partners. These beliefs and attitudes MUST change.

New York State has recently launched a yearlong, statewide public awareness campaign to fight domestic violence. The campaign is called, "Coaching Boys into Men". The goal is to engage men as partners in this fight because men have the opportunity and the responsibility to teach boys to respect girls and women. Society sends messages to boys to be tough and in control, to "be a man".

"Coaching Boys into Men" is a simple and basic concept. Be there and spend time with the boys in your life. They could be your son, your nephew, your grandson, your neighbor, or your younger brother. They could be the boys you teach or coach. They need your advice on how to behave towards girls. They learn by the example you set. Always treat women in a way your boy can admire.

There is a domestic violence shelter in Buffalo called the Haven House. The secret location of this shelter provides safety for women and children who have fallen victim to this silent killer. The Haven

House and shelters like it provide victims with the resources they need to rebuild their lives. The Haven House is funded by the United Way, the Department of Social Services, and other organizations.

The Buffalo Police took Jane and her children to the Haven House. She was also assisted by the Department of Social Services, Catholic Charities, and the Salvation Army.

Peace. That is all Jane wanted. Imagine the ripple effect of one small action taken against domestic violence. A man takes the time with one boy…talks to him about girls, women, and respect. He sets the example and paves the way. That boy grows up, marries, has a son, and does the same. Negative attitudes and beliefs can be changed one life at a time. This may take generations, but it *can* happen. If we choose to do nothing, we will be guilty of condoning and perpetuating this problem of domestic violence.

In response to my speech tonight, I ask you to become involved. Make it your business. Spend time with boys in your life and talk with them. Support the local charities that provide shelter, help, and services to women and children who are victims of domestic violence. Your support may be financial or through material donations. The Haven House is always in need of personal care items and other things for the shelter. The Haven House also accepts old cell phone donations that can be recycled to the victims of domestic violence.

If you suspect someone you know is being abused, approach her privately and ask her. She will not approach you or ask anyone out of fear. *Believe her.* Believe what she tells you is true. Offer help. Understand there are risks to every single decision a battered woman makes. Safety should be the number one concern.

In closing, Jane escaped her domestic violence because someone chose to become involved. She rebuilt her life with the help of local organizations. Years of counseling helped her to heal. She is now able to advocate for changes to help millions who suffer like she did. A ripple effect, one life at a time. She urges you to get involved.

I am Jane."[6]

The crowd responded with gasps of disbelief as I concluded my speech. They could not believe that

---

[6] Office of Child and Family Services, www.childfamilybny.org/Programs/HavenHouse;"Coaching Boys into Men" campaign, www.endabuse.org; National Coalition Against Domestic Violence, www.ncadv.org; New York State Office for the Prevention of Domestic Violence, www.opdv.state.ny.us; Verizon Foundation, www.foundation.verizon.com

I was the victimized woman in the story. I am an ordinary woman who has survived heartbreaking and terrifying events. Through all of it, I experienced an extraordinary God at work in my life. I have witnessed firsthand the depth of His love for me.

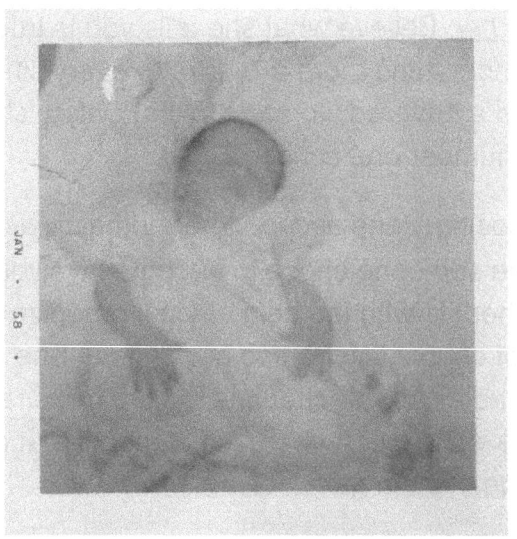

"You made all the delicate, inner parts of my body and knit me together in my mother's womb. Thank you for making me so wonderfully complex! Your workmanship is marvelous - and how well I know it. You watched me as I was being formed in utter seclusion, as I was woven together in the dark of the womb. You saw me before I was born. Every day of my life was recorded in your book. Every moment was laid out before a single day had passed." (Psalm 139:13-16)[7]

This psalm tells me that the heartbreaking events in my life were planned for me with purpose and intent. God does not make mistakes. In *"Experiencing God",* Henry Blackaby writes,

"Each of us has a unique pilgrimage with special insights and sensitivities that God can use in significant ways for His kingdom. No success or failure in our lives is wasted with God. He fashions the unique life to which He calls us, and then He is glorified when we live for Him. No life is ordinary when it is in the hands of our extraordinary God."[8]

I have survived a number of events that could have taken my life. God had a different plan for me. The road I have travelled has been uniquely designed for me. I endured a long process of physical, mental and emotional healing. During that healing process, I discovered the liberating power of forgiveness. The events of my life revealed an undeniable and undefeatable strength that was a direct result of my deeply rooted faith in God. I am an ordinary woman who loves and serves an

---

[7] New Living Translation: www.biblestudytools.com
[8] Henry Blackaby, Richard Blackaby, Claude King Experiencing God:Knowing and Doing the Will of God (Nashville, Tennessee: BH Publishing Group, 2008),283-284. Used by Permission.

extraordinary God. Walk with me as I share my story of heartbreak, survival, healing and blessing.

"The Lord himself goes before you and will be with you; he will never leave you nor forsake you. Do not be afraid; do not be discouraged." (Deut. 31:8)[9]

He was with me through it all. He went before me, walked beside me, held my hand, carried me and brought me through. Even in my darkest moments, I was not alone. Even when I felt I could not go on, His light showed me the way I should go.

---

9 Faith in Action Study Bible: Living God's Word in a Changing World (Grand Rapids, Michigan: Zondervan Corporation, 2001), 306.

Chapter Two

"Welcome to My World"

When I was a little girl, I loved to dream and pretend. My feet were firmly planted in reality as I used my creative imagination to conjure up the next adventurous dream. I had no difficulty entertaining myself if there was no one around to play with. Barbie dolls and matchbox cars were some of my favorites, as was throwing a blanket over the chain link fence in the backyard and riding my "horse". My horse and I would ride for hours to faraway places where we would encounter danger and adventure all wrapped up in an afternoon. My imagination was a wonderful place to spend time.

My neighborhood supplied many playmates. Because there were five Karens in the neighborhood, I was fondly named "Little Karen". I was very small for my age and the title was fitting. My friends and I would play for hours on end, at each others' houses and yards, having sleepovers, and playing at the playground at the end of the street. There were games of Red Rover, Dodge Ball, and the beloved Hide and Seek. After school, we would play until dinner. After dinner, we would play until darkness fell. All four seasons provided limitless hours of fun and laughter. In the spring, we flew kites. In the summer, we had water balloon fights, bicycle rides to Beaver Island State Park, and the Neighbor Days at the Catholic church. The fall leaves provided colored "rain" and "nests" to seek refuge in. The wet leaves in the ditch became "fish" that we caught with sticks. The winter cold and snow brought more adventures. We would build snow forts at the end of our driveways and have countless snowball fights. The snow also provided us with "mountains" at the end of the street. The snowplows and pay loaders would pile the snow ten to twelve feet high. They provided hours of endless fun in the snow. A pathway was created all along the top by the neighborhood kids. I remember having to leave early to walk to school because it was so much fun to walk the path along the top of the "mountain". The walk home was just as much fun, though we would linger longer. My imagination would kick into gear again, making up some adventure on that "mountain" as I made my way to and from school. There were arts and crafts at the playground, Saturday movies in the auditorium of the elementary school, parades, and block parties. I have wonderful memories of growing up there.

I did have one experience when I was four years old that I do not recall as well. My understanding of the situation has only come from hearing it through my mother and my siblings. I do remember the hospital bed. I had become seriously ill. Having contracted an evil combination of pneumonia and mononucleosis, I was confined to a hospital bed, packed in ice, with a high fever of 106 degrees. I was so near to death at one point, I am told, that my parents did not think they would be returning to the hospital to visit me. I do not have any details of how my status improved, but I believe that God moved in that situation and prayers were answered.

"This is what the Lord, the God of your father David, says: "I have heard your prayer and seen your tears; I will heal you." (2 Kings 20:5)[10]

God had a plan for my life. His angels kept vigil and God healed me from that near-death experience. Little did I know that this would not be the only time that His angels protected me and God's Hand lifted me from imminent danger.

As time passed and I grew older, my interests grew as well. My parents purchased a Wurlitzer organ and I began to take organ lessons. When I started, my feet could not even reach the pedals. I loved to play that Wurlitzer! I would practice for hours at a time, faithfully filling in my practice time log. I would sacrifice time with friends and other activities just for the sake of playing. My mother would just sit and listen. I had friends who would stand at the livingroom window and listen. For a time, I secretly kept the desire to attend the Juilliard School of Music and make something of my

---

10 Women of Faith Study Bible (Grand Rapids, Michigan: Zondervan Corporation, 2001), 612.

musical ambition. When I was thirteen, my cousin chose me to play the organ for her wedding. I flew to Michigan, where I played an enormous pipe organ in the balcony of her church on her special day. What a fantastic memory that is for me! I felt so honored and privileged to do that for her and her new husband. My years of playing also included many recitals and competitions, with trophies and ribbons to display for my efforts. I continued with my lessons until age seventeen, when my organ teacher asked me to be an instructor at his studio. In spite of the great opportunity that he was giving me, I was still only seventeen and I had other plans for my life. I turned him down. My time at the keys of my beloved Wurlitzer were winding down as other interests began to invade my time.

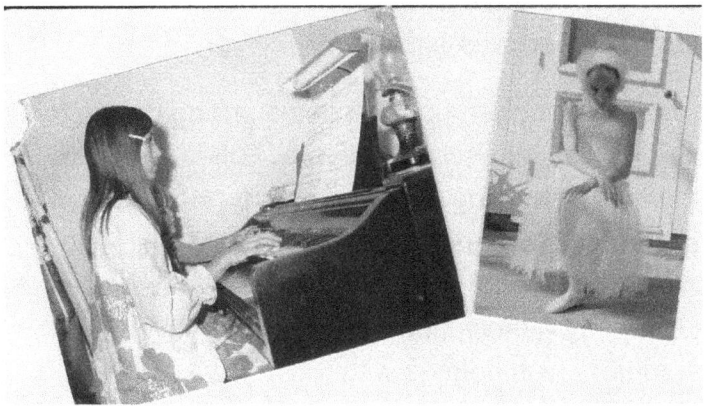

Another passionate interest that entered my life about the same time as the organ lessons was ballet. I loved to dance! I had a very strict ballet teacher whom I respected, feared and loved. Each and every lesson provided opportunity to improve and get stronger. Each year, I danced at the year-end recital which was an expression of all the skills we had learned that year. I remember loving the costumes, which were custom fit by a local seamstress. I also remember the makeup and false eyelashes, painstakingly applied perfectly by my sister. I enjoyed being on the stage with its bright lights and approving audiences. My dance lessons grew to include ballet, jazz, chechetti, and pointe. How I treasured my toe shoes! Before long, I was dancing six days a week. When my brother began college, my parents could no longer afford my expensive passion and my dance days were over. I completely understood the need at the time. My brother's education was more important and the family's need was greater.

As a teenager, I possessed a strong desire to help others, especially children. I often accepted the task of helping to raise funds for organizations such as the American Cancer Society, the American Lung Association, and the Muscular Dystrophy Association. A highlight of several of my summers was helping with the annual Lions Club picnic for blind children. I was also the neighborhood babysitter. Several families in the neighborhood relied on my dependability as well as the connections that I made with their children.

I feel that I was particularly blessed when it came to my friends. I had a few good friends that I could count on for true friendship. I am fortunate to maintain those friendships today. Of those friendships, there is one that stands head and shoulders above the others. She is a true friend who has provided limitless support and love for me since we were little girls. We have traveled a long road together, for which I am grateful. I am not certain that I could have survived some of the things I have, had it not been for her unwavering love and support. I wish everyone were as fortunate as I to have such a friend. On the other hand, I had another friend who had a profoundly negative influence on my life. I was in my early teens when I met her. My two year relationship with her took me down the wrong path, coerced me into making bad decisions, and ultimately ended with a life-changing event. I will explain more about that later. When it came to my teen years and a growing interest in boys, I met a boy when I was thirteen. His name was Jim and he stole my heart. We went out together for about two and half years. We talked on the phone for hours and met up at social events, especially the local hangout called the Help Center. I loved being with him. I felt special. Whenever his name came up in conversation or I saw him, it felt as though my heart skipped a beat. We shared the same circle of friends at the time, yet we eventually found ourselves wanting more than what that circle of friends could give us. We each made decisions to change our direction. Unfortunately, they were opposite directions. Sadly, we parted ways. Our paths would not cross again for many years.

    My family consists of my father, my mom, my sister, my brother and myself. My sister is ten years older than I am. We shared a room together. She always took care of me and watched over me. Some of my most treasured memories are with her and her bicycle. She had a wire basket on the front of her bicycle. She would put a blanket inside of it to cover the wires. I would sit in the basket and she would ride us around and show me off to her friends. I always had fun and eagerly looked forward to our next ride. My sister left home when I was only eight years old. I was heartbroken to see her go. She has lived long distances away from me since then, though we have worked hard to remain close. My brother is five years older that I am. We had a little more time together at home. There are two memories that I especially cherish when it comes to my brother. He could do a great impression of each of the Beatles. When he would tuck me in bed at night, I would request that he do his impressions and it would always make me smile and giggle. I also remember playing baseball with him in our backyard. We always had fun. Still, I was the "little sister" and I know there were times that he wished I would disappear! When he went away to college, I was heartbroken again. I was the only child left at home now.

My mother was a beautiful woman with black hair and brown eyes. She worked as a waitress for as long as I can remember. Mom worked hard at home taking care of the household and she worked long hours away from home to help make ends meet. I deeply respected the woman she was. We became exceptionally close through the years, particularly when it was only her and I at home. She was 52 years old when cancer took her life and I was the young age of twenty. The loss of my mother was desperately devastating. I give her the credit for my deep faith in God. She pressed to have us at church every week without fail and pushed us through religious instructions as well. As a teenager, I questioned why this was all necessary. She told me that when I was older I would be equipped to make my own decision concerning God. My mom had a deep faith in an unseen God. I wanted to experience that as well. Mom also had strength to endure difficult times. I was older when I realized that I had the same strength for the same reason.

Lastly, there was my father. He was a military man with the Navy for 22 years. Everything at home had to meet his impeccable standards. The authority he exerted over the household was uncomfortable and often frightening. Because he had an uncontrollable temper, there were often holes punched in the walls and broken household possessions. His uncontrollable fits of rage often escalated into physical abuse aimed at my mom, my sister, and my brother. I was his "baby" and for that reason, I was never on the receiving end of his abuse. Unfortunately, I witnessed plenty of it. There was one occasion particularly that I clearly remember, even though I was quite young at the time. He was unhappy with the meal that my mom had prepared. "Same old shit!" he yelled as he flipped over the entire kitchen table, sending all of its contents crashing to the floor. He stormed out of the house, squealed the car out of the driveway and drove away, leaving behind a crying family, broken dishes and an enormous mess. Growing up with my father living in the house exposed me to domestic violence and the physical, mental and emotional destruction that it leaves in its wake. If I could not go to a friend's house to escape the violence, I would hide in the closet or under my bed and cover my ears. When I was thirteen, my mom called all of us kids together and told us that she was getting a divorce. My immediate response was, "It's about time."

Chapter Three

"What is Domestic Violence?"

The New York State Office for the Prevention of Domestic Violence states that domestic violence "is a serious crime which often results in serious injury or even death." Even though statistics reflect that 97% of victims are women abused by males, domestic violence is not limited to women. This crime may happen to anyone "regardless of socio-economic status, race, ethnicity, age, education, employment status, physical ableness, marital status or childhood history."[11] Women, children, men, teens, elders, the disabled, gays and lesbians have all been found to experience this tragic behavior. Domestic violence can be physical abuse, emotional abuse or sexual abuse.

The following is a list of warning signs to look for if you or someone you love is being abused. Ask yourself the following questions:

- Does he/she keep telling you that you can never do anything right?

---

[11] New York State Office for the Prevention of Domestic Violence: www.opdv.state.ny.us

- Is he/she jealous of your friends and the time you spend away from him/her?
- Does he/she keep you or discourage you from seeing your friends or family members?
- Does he/she embarrass you or shame you with put-downs?
- Does he/she control all of the money spent in the household?
- Does he/she look at you or act in ways that scare you?
- Does he/she control or attempt to control who you see, where you go and what you do?
- Does he/she prevent you or attempt to prevent you from making your own decisions?
- Does he/she tell you that you are a bad parent and threaten to harm your children or take them away from you?
- Does he/she prevent you from working or attending school?
- Does he/she destroy your property and/or threaten to hurt or kill your pets?

- Does he/she intimidate you with the use of guns, knives and other weapons?

- Does he/she pressure you into having sex when you don't want to?

- Does he/she force you into doing things sexually that you are not comfortable with?

- Does he/she pressure you into using drugs or alcohol?

Physical abuse is defined as "an act of another party involving contact intended to cause feelings of physical pain, injury or other physical suffering or bodily harm."[12] Physical abuse can range from a simple slap to homicide. The following is a list of physically abusive behaviors:

- Pulling hair, slapping, kicking, punching, biting, pinching or choking you

- Withholding food, clothing, sleep or medicine

- Damaging property when they are angry, such as punching holes in walls, kicking doors, throwing and breaking things, etc.

- Using weapons to threaten you or hurting you with those weapons

---

[12] www.google.com

- Causing personal injury or broken bones
- Keeping you locked up in your home
- Preventing you from calling the police or seeking medical attention
- Hurting your children
- Driving recklessly or dangerously when you are in the car with them
- Abandoning you in an unfamiliar or dangerous place
- Forcing you to use drugs or alcohol
- Neglecting to take care of a child, elderly person, or ill/helpless partner that you have been given responsibility for

Emotional abuse is defined as "any act including confinement, isolation, verbal assault, humiliation, intimidation, infantilization, or any other treatment which may diminish the sense of identity, dignity and self-worth."[13] The following is a list of emotionally abusive behaviors:

- Calling you names, insulting you, mocking you and criticizing you
- Acting possessive and jealous

---

13 www.google.com

- Refusing to trust you
- Isolating you from your friends and family members
- Monitoring where you go, who you call and who you spend your time with
- Leaving nasty and demeaning messages for you
- Sending cruel letters and emails
- Demanding to know your whereabouts every minute
- Punishing you by withholding affection
- Threatening to hurt you, your children, your pets, or your family members
- Humiliating you, especially in front of others
- Blaming you for the abuse
- Gaslighting
- Accusing you of cheating on him/her
- Consistently cheating on you and blaming you for his/her actions
- Cheating on you intentionally to hurt you

- Cheating on you to prove they are more desirable than you are

- Controlling or attempting to control your appearance by approving or disapproving of your clothes, your perfume, your makeup, etc.

- Telling you that you will never find anyone better than him/her and that you are lucky to have him/her because no one else would want you

Sexual abuse is defined as "the forcing of unwanted sexual activity by one person on another, as by the use of threats or coercion; sexual activity that is deemed improper or harmful, as between an adult and a minor or with a person of diminished mental capacity." [14] The following is a list of sexually abusive behaviors:

- Forcing you to dress in a sexual way

- Insulting you in sexual ways or calling you sexual names

- Forcing you or manipulating you into performing sexual acts or favors

- Forcing you or manipulating you into having sexual intercourse

---

14 www.thefreedictionary.com

- Holding you down during sex
- Binding you during sex
- Hurting you with objects or weapons during sex
- Involving other people in sexual activities with you without your permission or against your will
- Ignoring your feelings about sex
- Forcing you to watch pornography
- Purposefully passing on a sexually transmitted disease to you
- Unwanted touching
- Rape

Why do men abuse women? The abusers use excuses such as "I lost my temper", "I had a bad day", and "I drank too much". I heard those excuses often. Remember, they are exactly that, excuses. Research shows that the underlying factor has to do with the abuser's attitudes and beliefs about the relationship between men and women. They believe that women are inferior, do not deserve respect, and should be controlled and overpowered.

The Domestic Violence Sourcebook explains that the abusers "seek control of the thoughts, beliefs, and conduct of their partners; restrict all of the victim's rights and freedoms; and punish their partner for breaking the rules or challenging their authority. Men who batter minimize the seriousness of their violence; believe they are entitled to control their partner; use anger, alcohol/drug use and stress as excuses for their behaviors; and blame the victim for their violence."

"A batterer covers up his violence by denying, minimizing, and blaming the victim. He often convinces his partner that the abuse is less serious than it is, or that it is her fault. He may tell her that "if only" she had acted differently, he wouldn't have abused her. Sometimes he will say "You made me do it."

Victims of abuse do not cause violence. The batterer is responsible for every act of abuse committed.

Domestic violence is a learned behavior. It is learned through: observation; experience; culture; family; community (peer group, school, etc.).

Abuse is not caused by: mental illness; genetics; alcohol and drugs; out-of-control behavior; anger; stress; behavior of the victim; problems in the relationship.

A batterer abuses because he wants to, and thinks he has a "right" to his behavior. He may think he is superior to his partner and is entitled to use whatever means necessary to control her."[15]

As my story unfolds, you will clearly see these patterns of attitude and behavior in my abusers. I was deeply moved as I read this information, feeling as though the author was writing about me and my life. I still find it frightening that the men who promised to love and cherish me became the beasts described here. According to the Office for the Prevention of Domestic Violence, "It is this belief (that they have a right), coupled with society's tolerance of domestic violence, that is at the root of domestic violence."[16] I experienced this tolerance firsthand. I can tell you that it is frightening. To hear people tell me that I deserved what I got, to hear them say that it is not their problem, and to walk away from what they see happening is simply deplorable. Attitudes and beliefs must change in order for this intimate crime to diminish.

---

[15] Sandra Judd (editor) Domestic Violence Sourcebook, 4th Edition (Detroit, Michigan:Omnigraphics, Inc., 2013), 20-21. Used by Permission.

[16] New York State Office for the Prevention of Domestic Violence: www.opdv.state.ny.us

Chapter Four

"Betrayal"

As we grow up and begin to take an interest in social activities, dating and romantic relationships, we need to be aware of what constitutes healthy and unhealthy relationships. I am referring to any relationship between two people, whether a platonic friendship or a romantic relationship. Some people may be fortunate to have positive, loving role models in their lives. Others may have to learn by trial and error, investing time and making mistakes. A healthy relationship allows you to be yourself. You are comfortable to do and say things that make you unique. There is mutual respect, trust, honesty and support. An unhealthy relationship will be marked with a lack of respect, mistrust, lying, lack of support and threatening behaviors. As teenagers, we tend to plunge headfirst into relationships, not giving any thought as to whether they are healthy or not. Nor do we give any thought to the outcomes or consequences of our choices in friends.

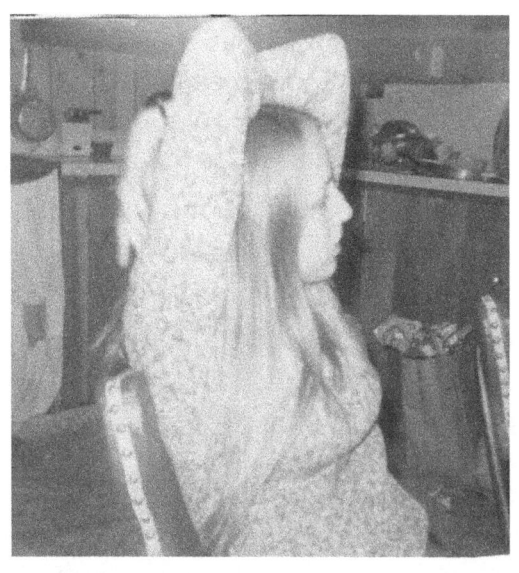

My friendship with Sierra began in my freshman year of high school. I was intrigued by her because she was popular and she had a unique way of standing out in a crowd. Her house was within walking distance of mine, so as our friendship developed, we began to spend time at each others' houses. I was naïve and trusting. I allowed Sierra into my naïve little world and I followed blindly as she taught me about her world. Sierra taught me about tampons, clothes, makeup, and David Bowie. She also taught me about marijuana, THC, mescaline and LSD. Sierra's world was all about having a good time, partying, dating, drugs, and sex. She had a boyfriend who belonged to a tough fraternity in Riverside. He and a number of his frat brothers were often at Sierra's house.

There were parties with drugs and alcohol. These were new experiences for me. My friendship with Sierra was fine for awhile. We shared some classes at school and we were often together after school. Because I knew that my mom did not approve of Sierra and my friendship with her, I began to lie to my mom. I hated lying to her. Sierra was coercing me down a path that I did not want to take, yet I saw no escape from this friendship. She had a strong hold over me.

One day after school, Sierra and I were at her house. We were in her room listening to some music after taking some THC. Sierra told me that she was going to get us a snack and she would be right back. I was unsuspecting as I sat on the floor looking at an album cover with my back to the door. The next thing I knew, Sierra's brother Kyle came in, grabbed me by the hair and literally dragged me across the house to his bedroom. On the way, we passed by three of his friends who were sitting on the couch laughing. Kyle threw me on the bed and proceeded to start locking the eight deadbolts that were on his two bedroom doors. Each time I tried to escape to one of the doors, he threw me on the bed again. With the room completely secured by the deadbolts, he ripped off my clothes, pinned me by my arms, and violently raped me. My screams and his friends laughing echoed in my ears.

When he was finished, he dressed and returned to his friends, triumphantly smiling about his victory. I quivered underneath the covers of the bed as Kyle's friend entered the room for his turn. He pulled the covers away to reveal my naked shaking body. He did not climb onto me as I anticipated he would. Instead, he used his large strong hands to feel his way painstakingly slowly, over my body for what seemed like hours. When he was satisfied that he had lingered long enough, he simply walked away. I could not move. I was frozen with fear. What would happen now? Would the next friend come in? Through my tears, I saw my innocence and my blood on the sheets of Kyle's bed. That is when he returned. He grabbed my hair, pulled me close and whispered in my ear, "If you tell anyone about this, I will let every one of the frat boys have their way with you." He let go.

I got off the bed, collected my clothes and went into the bathroom. I could not stop crying as I dressed and splashed some water on my face. I heard the telephone ring and Sierra answered. The person calling was my mom. I went to the phone, trying to keep my composure. I was late for dinner. I promised Mom that I was on my way and I hung up the phone. Sierra and Kyle had been standing right next to me, making certain that I did not tell Mom what had just happened. Sierra walked me home and cunningly asked my mom if she could sleep over. She wanted to assure my silence. I did not have much to say at all. The afternoon had been a life-changing and violent event that haunted me for years to come. I had nightmares. I was fearful. I slowly began to see less and less of Sierra until she finally disappeared from my life. I never told anyone about the events of that day for a very long time.

I was fourteen years old. I had no idea how to handle what had just happened to me. I spent a lot of time alone, crying, as I tried to think of what to do. I knew I could not tell anyone, for fear of retaliation. What if I got pregnant? The only thing I felt I could do at the time was to push it down deep, take one step at a time and move forward. That's what I did. I pushed it down deep. I took one step at a time. I moved forward. The fact remained that I was a victim of violence and I would never be the same again.

Sometimes, in our brokenness, all we can do is cry out to God and ask "Why?". Understanding God's plan can be very difficult in times like these. Understanding can be more difficult still, if you don't believe in a gracious and loving God. Nothing makes sense. Why do bad things happen to good people? The answer may be revealed somewhere down the road. We may not know the answer to that question on this side of heaven. Why does the star quarterback of the football team now have to spend his days fighting cancer? Why does a wonderful Christian family have to grieve the incomprehensible loss of their four year old son to a brain tumor? Why do people that we love and cherish so deeply take to illness or accident and die? Why does a young mother carry her healthy baby boy to 36 weeks, only to deliver her firstborn with no heartbeat? Why, in the innocence of my youth, did this happen to me?

God's Word tells us that He can use everything in our lives for our good, even the bad things. Especially the bad things.

"And we know that in all things God works for the good of those who love him, who have been called according to his purpose." (Romans 8:28)[17]

I loved God. Yet, I could not understand in my teenage mind how He could possibly bring good out of this situation. All I could feel was hurt, betrayal and shame.

In her book, "Loving God With All Your Mind", Elizabeth George writes, "He assures us that He controls all things, and He works all things for our good. This means we can look at each challenge and trial, each disappointment and tragedy life

---

[17] Women of Faith Study Bible (Grand Rapids, Michigan: Zondervan Corporation, 2001), 1860

brings as another opportunity to trust the Lord."[18] Elizabeth also explains that "God uses people, events and circumstances, both good and bad, to move us ultimately toward the fulfillment of His will and purpose for our lives. Everything – every person, every event – that touches us is for the purpose of making us like Christ. We can find comfort and hope as we navigate the maze of life when we remember the fact that God will use whatever He permits to happen to us to fulfill His purposes and to make us more like Jesus."[19]

I wanted to trust God to use even this unconscionable event for my good, but I could not comprehend why He would allow a "friend" to hurt me so badly. Where was God when Kyle and his friends were joyfully having their fun at my expense? In my fourteen year old mind, I simply could not see God in that situation. The pain that I held deep within me would simmer there for a very long time.

About 30 years later, under hypnosis and reliving that fateful day, my counselor asked me to look around the room to see Jesus. "I can't see

---

[18] Elizabeth George Loving God With All Your Mind (Eugene, Oregon: Harvest House Publishers, 1994/2005), 187. Used by Permission.

[19] Elizabeth George Loving God With All Your Mind (Eugene, Oregon: Harvest House Publishers, 1994/2005), 204. Used by Permission.

Him," I cried out over and over, as I frantically searched the room for Him. "He's there. Try," she gently encouraged me again. I looked around the room. "I can't see Him!" I cried out again. My counselor brought me back and ended our session for the day. She encouraged me to spend some quiet time seeking the answer. Emotionally drained, I drove to a quiet place and started to cry. I talked to God and told Him that I really needed to know where He was that day when Kyle was raping me and no one came to save me. In the quiet stillness of those moments, I clearly heard God say, "I was holding your hand."

Chapter Five

"The Dating Game"

When we read or listen to the media these days, the news is filled with stories of violence. This is the age we live in. When it comes to domestic violence, the areas of abuse that have rising statistics are teen dating violence and college campus violence. The seriousness of this problem of dating violence is explained in this way:

- "In the United States alone, one in three adolescent girls (35%) is a victim of interpersonal violence

- 80% of teens say they know someone who has been controlled by a partner, and 60% know someone who has been physically abused. 29% of teens say that they themselves have been physically abused by a dating partner, and 54% report some form of abuse – yet only 37% of parents are aware that their child has been abused in some way.

- 47% of 13-18 year olds who have been in relationships reported that they have personally been victimized by controlling behaviors from a boyfriend or girlfriend.

- Dating violence can have a negative effect on health throughout life. Teens who are victims are more likely to be depressed and do poorly in school. They may engage in unhealthy behaviors, like using drugs and alcohol, and are more likely to have eating disorders. Some teens even think about or attempt suicide. Teens who are victims in high school are at a higher risk for victimization during college.

- One in four teens who have been in a serious relationship say their boyfriend or girlfriend has tried to prevent them from spending time with friends or family; the same number have been pressured to only spend time with their partner.

- Almost one third of girls who have been in a relationship (29%) said they've been pressured to have sex or to engage in sexual acts when they didn't want to do so.

- Nearly 80% of females reported experiencing at least one incident of physical or sexual aggression by the end of college.

- 49% of males (high school to fourth year of college) report using at least one incident of physical or sexual violence against an intimate partner."[20]

Loveisrespect.org reports, "Nearly 1.5 million high school students nationwide experience physical abuse from a dating partner in a single year. One in ten high school students have been purposefully hit, slapped or physically hurt by a boyfriend or girlfriend. One fourth of high school girls have been victims of physical or sexual abuse. Approximately 70% of college students say they have been sexually coerced."[21]

Teen dating violence is defined as "physical, sexual or psychological/emotional violence within a dating relationship. As teen develop emotionally, they are heavily influenced by their relationship experiences. Healthy relationship behaviors can have a positive effect on a teen's emotional development. Unhealthy, abusive or violent relationships can cause short-term and long-term

---

20 New York State Office for the Prevention of Domestic Violence: www.opdv.state.ny.us

21 www.loveisrespect.org

negative effects or consequences to the developing teen."[22]

"Most friendships, acquaintances and dates never lead to violence, of course. But, sadly, sometimes it happens. When forced sex occurs between two people who already know each other, it is known as date rape or acquaintance rape.

Even if two people know each other well, or even if they were intimate or had sex before, no one has the right to force a sexual act on another person against his or her will.

Although it involves forced sex, rape is not about sex and passion. Rape has nothing to do with love. Rape is an act of aggression and violence.

You may hear some people say that those who have been raped were somehow "asking for it" because of the clothes they wore or the way they acted. That's wrong. The person who is raped is not to blame. Rape is always the fault of the rapist. And that's also the case when two people are dating – or even in an intimate relationship. One

---

[22] Sandra Judd (editor) Domestic Violence Sourcebook, 4th Edition (Detroit, Michigan: Omnigraphics, Inc., 2013), 190. Used by Permission.

person never owes the other person sex. If sex is forced against someone's will, that's rape."[23]

There are a number of ways you can protect yourself. Take a self-defense class. These are available for a reasonable fee. You can learn skills that will allow you to disable your attacker and free you to escape. You should avoid secluded places or being alone with someone who makes you feel uncomfortable. Always be aware of your surroundings. When you are with a group of friends, watch out for each other. Never walk alone. Try to have at least one friend with you. The buddy system usually works.

The US Department of Justice estimates that "one in every six women has been raped at one time. In a single year, more than 300,000 women and almost 93,000 men are estimated to have been raped. Female teens are most likely to be sexually assaulted by intimate partners and acquaintances, while adult women were at greatest risk from their intimate partners. In comparison, male victims of all ages were most at risk from acquaintances."[24]

---

[23] Sandra Judd (editor) Domestic Violence Sourcebook, 4th Edition (Detroit, Michigan: Omnigraphics, Inc., 2013), 210. Used by Permission.

[24] New York State Office for the Prevention of Domestic Violence: www.opdv.state.ny.us

What should you do if you have been a victim of a sexual assault? First and foremost, think of your safety. Go to a place where you feel safe and are away from danger. Talk to someone you trust. You should seek medical attention immediately. Keep in mind that your body and clothes are evidence. You should leave everything just the way it is. Do not change your clothes, comb your hair, brush your teeth, eat, drink, or bathe. Your first inclination may be to strip down and get in the shower to scrub away all of the filth. That would be a mistake. Report your assault to campus security or to a local law enforcement agency.

College students can face some unique challenges because they are often living away from home and in campus housing. Because of the higher incidence of drug and alcohol use on the college campuses, these can be factors in sexual assaults on campus. More often than not, victims are fearful to report a rape if drugs or alcohol have been involved. When living on campus, it is also more difficult to escape the one who assaulted you because of shared classes or residence living. Resident life staff and campus security can be a place to turn to for assistance.

If you are interested in learning more about dating, healthy relationships, how to help or get help, explanations of dating abuse, and public awareness of dating violence, go to loveisrespect.org. This is a fantastic website, full of information for teens and college students. Parents may find useful information there as well, as it provides great topics for serious discussions with your dating daughter or son.

Chapter Six

"Love Hurts"

I was nineteen when I met Jeffrey. I was at a bar with my friends, playing pool and having a good time. Jeffrey was a regular at the bar because everyone knew him. He liked to impress everyone with his fancy Corvette and his wallet stuffed full of cash. He was employed as an electrician with a local company. We started dating and our relationship quickly grew serious. After a few short months, we were engaged to be married. I did not pay too much attention to his occasional outbursts of temper or to the fact that he spent so much of his time and money at the bar. I naively thought his outbursts were due to drinking too much that night or that he had a short fuse. I thought his presence at the bar was something that would change when we got married. I did not see either as being a problem. There is a saying that states, "Love is blind". This was truly the case when it came to Jeffrey. Little did I know the path that I would blindly journey before my eyes were opened.

We were in the midst of wedding plans, with only a short time before our big day, when we received the terrible news. My mom had been diagnosed with stage four lung cancer and the prognosis was months. Suddenly, everything was different. I wanted "my day" to be a special day for her, full of love, family and wonderful memories. I believe that it was. We had a special song for her during the ceremony, six of her seven siblings attended, and she looked beautiful.

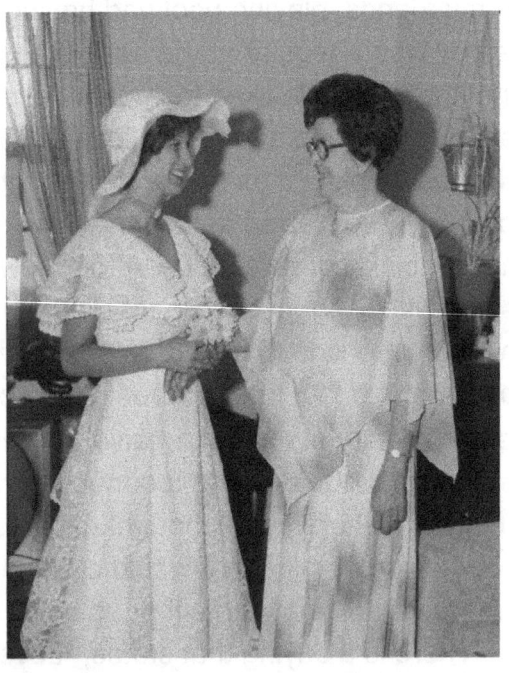

Jeffrey and I went to the Pocono Mountains for our honeymoon. A honeymoon should be full of wonderful memories and fun times as the couple begins their new life together. Our honeymoon was fraught with emotion and intense arguments. On our wedding night, I was rudely awakened by a full blown punch right in the middle of my back. He claimed to have had a bad dream.

Jeffrey did not think anything of mocking and ridiculing me in front of other couples as we participated in activities like miniature golf and dance lessons. I clearly recall returning to our apartment after our honeymoon. There was no carrying of the bride over the threshold. Jeffrey went in first and I followed. The door closed behind me and I was terrified. I had goose bumps. I was alone with a man that I had chosen to spend my life with. I was frozen in my tracks for a moment as I asked myself, "What have I done?"

The next few months were filled with anguish as I worked full-time, took care of our apartment, and helped to care for my quickly deteriorating mother. Jeffrey was less than supportive. His anger burned as he said hurtful things that crushed my spirit nearly as much as watching my mom die before my tear-filled eyes and broken heart. We lost her in December, only six months after her diagnosis and just weeks before Christmas. No loss in my life has been more difficult.

The physical abuse began eight short months later, when our firstborn son was only six weeks old. The bar across the street from our apartment was emptying of loud and obnoxious partygoers around midnight. Jeffrey became clearly agitated as the noise continued. His anger finally reached a point where he could no longer contain it and he lashed out at me. He slapped and punched me and put his hands around my neck, choking me. Suddenly, without a word, he stopped and walked away.

The next day, I was covered with bruises from his blows. As I looked in the mirror, the handprints around my neck were clearly visible. When I opened the bathroom door, Jeffrey was standing there. He was full of apology, promising he would never do it again and professing his undying love for me. Somehow, I believed him. I believed he was sorry and I believed that he loved me. At that time, I also held firmly to the belief that when you marry, your husband will love you and take care of you. I was 21 years old. My mom was gone, my siblings were far away, my relationship with my father was nonexistent and I was not prepared to face the world alone. I took Jeffrey at his word.

From my own personal experiences as well as my research, I can tell you that there are three stages to the cycle of abuse. The first stage is the tension building stage. The thoughts and feelings inside the abuser are escalating and he is looking for someone to blame these feelings on. For example, in the first abusing incident with Jeffrey, he was initially irritated by the noise level of the partygoers across the street. As his irritation grew to anger, he began to punch the couch cushions and throw things. When he could no longer contain his anger, he began hurting me. The second stage of the cycle of abuse is the actual abusing incident. Picture a teapot, if you will, on the burner slowly heating until the water boils. When it is boiling, and can no longer contain itself, the teapot blows off steam and whistles. This abusing incident can take many different forms and last for only moments, or continue for hours or even days. The third stage in the cycle is called "the honeymoon phase". The abuser is extremely loving and apologetic, asking forgiveness and full of promises to never hurt you again. He really believes what he is saying. He is tender and may even help take care of your injuries. He is very convincing. When you are completely convinced of his sincerity, you accept his apology, believe his promises and perhaps even believe his justification for the abuse. Everything is peaceful and wonderful again.

This cycle will repeat itself over and over again and will usually become more frequent and severe. I believe that this cycle of abuse is what the general public does not understand. This is why a woman cannot "just leave". She is caught in this cycle and becomes more deeply engaged in it as time goes on.

Jeffrey's drinking became more and more of a problem until its ramifications permeated every area of his life. There were problems in his relationships, his health, our marriage and his job. He would pass out on the patio, on the bathroom floor and in his car. He began to miss work and that is when his employer stepped in to help. Jeffrey entered a six week detox program at a local hospital through a benefit provided by his employer. I attended Al-Anon meetings to help with my understanding of alcoholism and my part in recovery. My Al-Anon book "One Day at a Time" became as important as my Bible. Jeffrey became sober and began to live a different life once he was discharged from the hospital.

Our marriage improved for awhile. We moved from our apartment and bought a house. Suddenly, without warning, Jeffrey started drinking again. He became verbally and physically abusive again. This time, the abuse did not stay within the boundaries of our closed doors. We had arguments in front of his friends and our neighbors. He always made me look like the one who was wrong. *I* made him do what he did. *I* pushed him to drink. *I* made him hurt me. Jeffrey's friends were unsympathetic to my situation. They would say things like, "It can't be that bad, you're still here" and "You must like it because you stay with him". Their attitudes and comments of indifference and ignorance hurt me deeply.

With his absenteeism increasing at work again, Jeffrey's company stepped in again. They put him through the detox program a second time. Jeffrey became sober a second time. Shortly afterward, we had a second son. I wanted to believe that everything would be fine. Our lives had been so tumultuous to this point. Unfortunately, this period of sobriety would be short-lived. Jeffrey did not seem to have the willpower to stay sober, even with so much at stake and so much to lose. Little issues became big issues. Molehills became mountains.

Jeffrey maintained control with me by the looks, gestures and actions he made. They were like a silent, private language he used in the presence of others. I knew how to decipher those looks and gestures. I knew what was coming when we were alone again.

As his wife, Jeffrey had certain expectations of me. Dinner had to be served hot and on the table at exactly 5:00 pm. The house had to be spotless. The clean laundry had to be ironed, including underwear and bed sheets. The boys always had to look neat and fresh. I always had to look and smell nice for him. If I failed to meet any of these expectations on any given day, he beat me. Because I was a homemaker and did not work outside of the home, I depended on Jeffrey for money for groceries and household needs. His need for control had escalated to the point where he forced me to play poker with him or perform a strip tease for him just to get money for groceries. If I lost at poker or he did not like my strip tease, he would just say, "Too bad" and laugh. Jeffrey always wanted sex when he wanted it, no matter what else was going on at the time. If I was not a willing participant, he would beat me and rape me. Most times when this happened, he kept a knife at my throat or a gun to my head until I pleased him.

Elaine Weiss, Ed.D, author of "Family and Friends' Guide to Domestic Violence" explains, "If you want to comprehend the incomprehensible, you must conceive of a home where there is a rule about everything…and the rules keep changing. You must imagine a relationship where differences of opinion are never tolerated and compromises are never negotiated. You must picture a man who insists that he be obeyed at all times, immediately and without question. You must visualize a woman who puts all her energy into "getting it right". Only there is no way she can ever get it right. Because he needs her to get it wrong." [25]

This was my life with Jeffrey. Day after day, month after month, I expended all of my energy to

---

[25] Elaine Weiss, Ed.D Family and Friends Guide to Domestic Violence: How to Listen, Talk and Take Action When Someone You Care About is Being Abused (Volcano, California: Volcano Press, inc., 2003), 13. Used by Permission.

follow the "rules" and be the "perfect" wife. This was my life for four years. On one occasion in particular, I took a severe beating. I needed medical attention. Jeffrey had picked me up over his head and thrown me across the living room. The right side of my jaw had hit squarely on the corner of the door opening. I could not take any more. I ran from the house with Jeffrey chasing after me, yelling, "Run!" and laughing. I had never known such fear as I did on that day when I was literally running for my life.

With the help of my caring neighbors, Anielka and Stanislaw, I received the medical attention that I needed. Out of their concern, they did not want me to return home. I stayed with them for a couple days while they nursed and tended to me. I had to have most of my food in liquid form and my wounds tended to. During that time, all I could think of was my little boys. They were still there with him. They were my life and all that I had to cling to. How could I think of not returning? I went back home.

Jeffrey offered more apologies, but he made me pay for the mistake of running away. He completely cut me off from the outside world. He took my car off the road. He took my driver's license. He turned off the telephone, stopped the mail and stopped the newspaper. If I went anywhere with the boys, I pulled them in a little red wagon. The neighbors watched the house while Jeffrey was gone at work and reported any and all activity to him when he returned. I was a prisoner in my own home. I never felt so alone.

Chapter Seven

"Why Stay?"

The National Coalition Against Domestic Violence has published an article by Susan G.S. McGee entitled, "20 Reasons Why She Stays". Susan McGee writes, "Some battered women are held prisoner in their own homes. Assailants use psychological terrorism and brainwashing techniques to keep them in the violent relationship."

"Take a look at the "Stockholm Syndrome", often used as an explanatory model by law enforcement. The hostages identify with, become attached to, and take the side of their captors. Studies have found that members of the following groups have suffered from the "Stockholm Syndrome" – concentration camp survivors; prisoners of war; physically and/or emotionally abused children; battered women; civilians in Chinese Communist prisons; cult members; women and youth trapped in prostitution; women and youth trafficked internationally. The Stockholm Syndrome is valuable in describing the systematic methods used to break down the victims' will to resist and bring them under control. It is also valuable in explaining how the responses of those who are victimized – which may seem incomprehensible – become easily understandable survival reactions in life-threatening, abusive situations. "

"Emotional abuse occurs in virtually all relationships where physical violence exists. The assailant will use extremely derogatory, often sexually explicit epithets tailored to the vulnerabilities of the survivor. He will employ knowledge gained in an intimate relationship to attack the woman's spirit and sense of her own value. This constant barrage of verbal abuse wears down the woman's resistance, making it more difficult for her to leave."

"Psychological terrorism goes far beyond name-calling and vicious verbal attacks. It may involve withholding food and water, sleep deprivation, withholding medication, administering drugs and medication, total isolation, degradation, "gaslighting", Russian Roulette, demonstrations that the batterer is "all powerful", occasional reinforcements for compliant behavior, and frustrating any attempts at non-compliance."

"Rape, sexual abuse and sexual humiliation are routine in battering relationships. This is another tactic habitually practiced by hostage takers and those who run concentration camps. Because sexuality is such a potentially intimate and sacred experience, sexual abuse and domination are particularly degrading to the spirit and weaken the capacity to resist."[26]

According to the Alabama Coalition Against Domestic Violence, there are many reasons why an abused woman will stay in the relationship. Some of them include:

"Economic Reasons:

- few job skills
- limited education or work experience
- limited cash
- no access to bank account
- fear of poverty

Pressure from Community of Faith/Family:

- family expectation to stay in marriage "at any cost"
- family denial of violence
- family blame her for violence
- religion may disapprove of divorce

---

[26] Susan G.S. McGee 20 Reasons Why She Stays, National Coalition Against Domestic Violence: www.ncadv.org

- religious leader may tell her to "stay and pray"

Guilt/Self-Doubt:

- guilt about failure of the relationship
- guilt about choosing an abuser
- feelings of personal incompetence
- concern about independence
- loneliness

Concern for children:

- abuser may charge her with " kidnapping" or sue for custody
- abuser may abduct or abuse the children
- questions whether she can care for and support children on her own
- fears losing custody of her children
- believes children need a father

Lack of Community Support"

- unaware of services available to battered women
- lack of adequate child care

- few jobs
- negative experiences with service providers
- lack of affordable housing
- isolated from community services
- no support from family and friends"[27]

When I thought about leaving, I faced a number of the issues on this list. I had no access to our bank accounts; I was not employed and did not have a source of income without Jeffrey; I was afraid of living on the street in poverty; I felt guilty for marrying an abuser; I had deep feelings of incompetence; I questioned whether or not I had the ability to take care of my boys and properly provide for their needs; I feared losing custody of them; I was unaware of services that were available to me; I had no one to help me take care of my boys; I was not sure I could find a place to live that was affordable; and I had no immediate support from family or friends. I was alone and lost.

During that time of desperate isolation, I turned to the Bible. My Bible was one thing that Jeffrey did not touch. He had broken or destroyed nearly everything else of value that I loved, including my

---

[27] Alabama Coalition Against Domestic Violence: www.acadv.org

35mm camera. Psalm 91 became my lifeline. All I could do was cling to those words and hope and pray that this great and distant God would hear my cries.

"He who dwells in the shelter of the Most High will rest in the shadow of the Almighty. I will say of the Lord, "He is my refuge and my fortress, my God, in whom I trust." Surely he will save you from the fowler's snare and from the deadly pestilence. He will cover you with his feathers, and under his wings you will find refuge; his faithfulness will be your shield and rampart. You will not fear the terror of the night, nor the arrow that flies by day, nor the pestilence that stalks in the darkness, nor the plague that destroys at midday. A thousand may fall at your side, ten thousand at your right hand, but it will not come near you. You will only observe with your eyes and see the punishment of the wicked. If you make the Most High your dwelling – even the Lord, who is my refuge – then no harm will befall you, no disaster will come near your tent. For he will command his angels concerning you to guard you in all your ways; they will lift you up in their hands, so that you will not strike your foot against a stone. You will tread upon the lion and the cobra; you will trample the great lion and the serpent. "Because he loves me," says the Lord, "I will rescue him; I will protect him, for he acknowledges my name. He will call upon me, and I will answer him; I will be with him in trouble, I will deliver him and honor him. With long life will I satisfy him and show him my salvation." (Psalm 91:1-16)[28]

Jeffrey began to sit next to the bed at night as I tried to go to sleep. In his attempt to deprive me of sleep, he held a baseball bat in his hands and smiled. I clutched my Bible to my chest, praying and believing that God would save me and allow me to see another day. One night, Jeffrey was forcing himself on me and holding a gun to my head. We were in the front hallway on the floor and the front door was open. I started screaming, "Someone help me!" After a couple of screams and Jeffrey's punches, a neighbor called out, "Can I help you?" Jeffrey yelled back, "Mind your own f***ing business!" He closed the door and said, "If you had not screamed, I would not have to do this." He beat me and raped me at gunpoint because I screamed.

After a month of being held captive, I tried to start formulating a way to get help. My attempts at formulating a plan were feeble, at best, because I did not even know where to begin. I needed someone to know what I was going through. I needed someone to help me. Although my caring neighbors, Anielka and Stan, knew something was

---

[28] Women of Faith Study Bible (Grand Rapids, Michigan: Zondervan Corporation, 2001), 956.

going on, they were elderly and did not know what to do. They put a Bible on the front porch. Jeffrey picked it up and laughed. He set it on fire and threw it on Anielka and Stan's driveway. The Bible did not burn.

I could not have anticipated what would happen next, in spite of all of the abuse I had suffered. Jeffrey cornered me in the back room and doused me with lighter fluid. I started screaming as Jeffrey laughed and lit a match. He threw it at me, but the flame went out. I was still screaming and trying to push past him. He pushed me back into the corner, laughed and lit another match. At that moment, God stepped in. There was a knock at the front door. There were four police officers there. Not waiting for a response, they entered the house. They forced Jeffrey to sit on the couch. The officers instructed me to pack a bag, get my boys, and they would take us to a safe place. My hands were shaking and tears were streaming down my cheeks as I packed a bag and collected my boys from their room. I do not know who called the police that day. If they had not arrived when they did, I am certain that I would have become another domestic violence homicide statistic. Four officers felt like an army. They were larger than life. I looked out the window of the police car and breathed a sigh of relief. I was finally safe. This time, I had my precious little boys with me. *We* were finally safe.

Chapter Eight
"How to Help"

Is there someone in your life who is a victim of domestic violence? Considering the statistics that one in four women suffers from domestic violence, I am certain that you know *someone*. Perhaps this person is a neighbor, a work associate, a classmate or a family member. Do you want to make a difference for this person? In order to help, you must first examine your attitudes concerning domestic violence. Some people choose *not* to help because they feel that it is none of their business. Unfortunately, choosing *not* to step in could further endanger her. She will remain isolated and silent, perpetuating the endless cycle of violence with no means of escape. If you *do* choose to help her, you should commit wholeheartedly to doing whatever it takes. If you are close to the abuser as well, you need to remember that abusers are skilled manipulators. Jeffrey was very skilled at manipulating family and friends into believing his stories of what "really" happened. He would tell them that I fell down the stairs, that I walked into the wall because I wasn't watching where I was going, and that I was accident-prone. Family and friends were easily taken in and missed what was really going on for a long time. Of course, if he was telling the story in my presence, there was no way that I could refute it.

How can you know for certain that she is being abused? The answer is two-fold and simple. First, *ask her.* Ask her directly and privately. She needs to know that she can trust you completely or she will not be truthful. Fear, embarrassment, judgment and blame are just a few reasons that she may not give a truthful answer. I wish someone had asked me. I remember feeling embarrassed, trying to hide my bruises and black eyes with turtlenecks and makeup. I remember having fear completely overwhelm and paralyze me whenever we were with people. What would people think? Would they think that I deserved it? Would they react the same way that Jeffrey's friends did by saying, "It can't be that bad, you're still here," and "You must like it because you stay with him"? Second, *believe her.* Believe what she tells you because it is true, no matter how much you may not want to believe it. What she shares with you will take a great deal of courage on her part. You need to understand the risks that she is taking by telling you. Looking back, I honestly do not know how the path I travelled would have changed if someone had asked me. The people who cared the most about me lived long distances away. There was nothing they could do for me. There *were* people close by that could have helped if they had chosen to. I just wish someone had cared enough to ask me.

According to the New York State Office for the Prevention of Domestic Violence, the following are possible indicators of domestic violence:

- Visible physical injury including: bruises, lacerations, burns, human bite marks, and fractures – especially of the eyes, nose, teeth and jaw; injuries during pregnancy, miscarriage, or premature births; unexplained delay in seeking treatment for injuries; and multiple injuries in different stages of healing.

- Illnesses that may be related to battering include: stress-related illnesses such as headaches, backaches, chronic pain, gastrointestinal disorders, sleep disorders, eating disorders, and fatigue; anxiety-related conditions such as heart palpitations, hyperventilation, and "panic attacks"; and less commonly, depression, suicidal thoughts or attempts, and alcohol or other drug problems.

- "Presenting problems" are often related to or a result of domestic violence and include: marital or "family" problems; alcohol or other drug addictions; and "mental health" problems.

- In the workplace, the effects of domestic violence can emerge as: lost productivity, chronic absenteeism or lateness, or request for excessive amounts of time off; on-the-job harassment by the abuser, either in person or over the phone; and poor employment history, or loss of employment.[29]

I can tell you that I displayed the visible signs of bruises, lacerations, and multiple injuries in different stages of healing. I suffered from frequent

---

[29] New York State Office for the Prevention of Domestic Violence: www.opdv.state.ny.us

headaches, stomach upsets, sleep disorders, fatigue, "panic attacks", and at times, depression from the complete sense of hopelessness that I felt. During the days of the most intense abuse, my petite frame dropped to an unbelievable 85 pounds. How people could not see what was happening is beyond my comprehension, although I have come to believe that they simply chose not to. This is the attitude that is contributing to the social tolerance that perpetuates domestic violence. Believing that it is not our business or that someone else will do something about it denies responsibility. We *all* have a responsibility.

"Finally, all of you, live in harmony with one another; be sympathetic, love as brothers, be compassionate and humble. Do not repay evil with evil or insult with insult, but with blessing, because to this you were called so that you may inherit a blessing." (1 Peter 3:8-9)[30]

I have overheard many a conversation shared between people who do not understand that domestic violence is about power and control. I have heard the comment "Why doesn't she just leave?" more than I care to. Leaving is a process and not just a single event. The one who is being abused cannot "just leave". The average battered

---

30 Women of Faith Study Bible (Grand Rapids, Michigan: Zondervan Corporation, 2001), 2027.

woman will leave and return seven to eight times before she leaves permanently. There are so many things to consider. Above everything, safety is the most important.

Aside from being there for her, there are a number of additional ways you can help. You can be instrumental in helping her to develop a safety plan. You can help her find resources and point her in the right direction to get assistance. You can support and participate in public awareness campaigns. Every state has a domestic violence website that contains a wealth of information about abuse and assistance. Go to the website with her or encourage her to check it out on her own. For safety purposes, each website contains an immediate escape button in case of danger. See Appendix.

Another way that you can help fight domestic violence is to participate in the HopeLine Cell Phone Drive sponsored by Verizon. Started in 1995, the Verizon HopeLine Program recycles and/or refurbishes cell phones and equipment, in an environmentally friendly way, to be redistributed to domestic violence programs and other organizations that serve victims in need. Organizing a cell phone drive is simple and easy to do. All cell phones and equipment that are collected can easily be dropped off at a Verizon HopeLine donation box in your community.

Chapter Nine

"Public Awareness"

The purpose of public awareness campaigns on domestic violence is to educate the community about the prevalence of abuse, encourage people to take action, as well as alert survivors concerning options and resources that are available to them.

The Purple Ribbon campaign uses the purple ribbon as a unifying symbol of courage, survival, honor and dedication to ending domestic violence. In addition to demonstrating support for victims and advocates, the display of these purple ribbons throughout a community can convey a powerful message that there is no place for domestic violence in their homes, neighborhoods, places of work or schools. Each year, the month of October is designated to be "Domestic Violence Awareness Month." The campaign slogan is "Shine the Light on Domestic Violence". This is when you may see the most display of the purple ribbons.

The Clothesline Project originated with 31 shirts in Hyannis, Massachusetts in 1990 through the Cape Cod Women's Agenda. A small group of women, many of whom had experience with domestic violence themselves, designed the visual monument as an educational tool to help transform staggering statistics of domestic violence against women and children. The decision to use a clothesline came about when the women realized they often exchanged information over their backyard fences while hanging laundry.

In 1990, a group of women artists and writers became alarmed with the growing number of domestic violence homicides in their state of Minnesota. To commemorate the lives of the 26 women who were murdered that year, they created 26 free-standing, life-sized red wooden figures, each bearing the name of a woman who once lived among them. Each woman's life violently ended at the hands of a husband, ex-husband, partner or acquaintance. A twenty-seventh figure was added to the display to represent the uncounted women whose murders were unsolved or erroneously ruled as accidental. The women who organized this public awareness campaign called the figures of the display "Silent Witnesses".

On September 26, 1999, Gladys Ricard was murdered by her abusive former boyfriend on the day she was supposed to marry her fiancé. Two years later, the Gladys Ricard and Victims of Domestic Violence Memorial Walk began. Participating women march in wedding dresses or all in white as this annual event memorializes the victims of domestic violence and raises community awareness of the seriousness of this crime.

Domestic violence is a deadly crime that leaves a painful emptiness, a permanent empty place at the table, for the families whose loved ones were killed at the hands of their abusers. The Women's Resource Center in Scranton, Pennsylvania organized this "Empty Place at the Table" campaign in the 1990's. This unique exhibit comprises victims' place settings, photographs and personal items, such as a child's favorite toy or a woman's scarf, as well as newspaper clippings about their homicide.

Public awareness campaigns such as "Coaching Boys into Men", that I referred to in my speech, are vitally necessary for teaching boys how to treat women with respect and dignity. As explained on the New York State Office for the Prevention of Domestic Violence website, "the goal of the campaign is to engage men as partners in the fight against domestic violence. The message of the campaign is that boys learn from the men in their lives. As a father, coach, mentor or male friend, men have the opportunity – and the responsibility – to teach boys to respect girls and women. They're watching; they're waiting; they'll listen."[31]

An award winning public awareness campaign in New York State in 2006 was called "Real Men. Real Respect for Women". This campaign was directed at young men and encouraged them to stand up to someone that was being abusive in the fight against teen dating violence. The slogan of the campaign, "If it doesn't feel right, it probably isn't" spoke directly to the young victims of the increasing violence of teen dating.

Another teen dating violence campaign distributed flyers to mall kiosks in the hopes of reaching teenage mall shoppers. The campaign slogan reflected on the flyers was "You Are Not His Property".

In the "Domestic Violence, It's Not a Game" campaign, New York State enlisted the assistance of New York Giants football player Tiki Barber. His radio announcements were directed at men and "made the distinction between power over one's opponent on the football field and the much more appropriate sharing of power in a personal relationship." Perhaps in light of the recent NFL

---

[31] New York State Office for the Prevention of Domestic Violence: www.opdv.state.ny.us

domestic violence issues, this campaign should be back in the forefront.

"This Isn't Love" was another teen dating violence awareness and prevention campaign. This campaign engaged social media and electronic distribution. The intention of the campaign was to encourage teens to think about some of the behaviors they were experiencing or inflicting, such as jealousy or possessiveness, and make them realize these are not behaviors associated with love and a healthy relationship. Quite the opposite, they are signs of control and forms of abuse.

In 2014, February was designated as Teen Dating Violence Awareness and Prevention Month in New York State. They used their "Send a Candy Heart" campaign to raise awareness of the increasing statistics of teen dating violence. Sadly, according to New York State Office for the Prevention of Domestic Violence, in the United States alone, approximately one in three adolescent girls will be a victim of interpersonal violence. That is a mind-boggling 35% of all adolescent girls. This "Send a Candy Heart" campaign used social media to encourage teens as well as adults to send a candy heart pledging specific ways they will work to end dating violence. "Candy hearts are supposed to be fun, sweet and good, just like healthy relationships. Too often teens receive negative messages about relationships or are with partners who tear them down. Our goal is to send messages pledging to support victims and to work to end teen dating violence. Sending a candy heart lets everyone on your social media know you're aware of and concerned about dating violence – also that you're there to help if they need it."[32]

You can participate in public awareness campaigns to help raise awareness by distributing public education materials to your local library, your doctor's office, your hair salon, to your colleagues at work, or to clubs where you belong. Materials can be downloaded free of charge from the domestic violence websites. See Appendix.

Educating the public at the national, state and local levels is the key to changing behaviors, beliefs and statistics. I encourage you to be responsible and do whatever you can to help with this fight against domestic violence.

---

[32] New York State Office for the Prevention of Domestic Violence: www.opdv.state.ny.us

Chapter Ten
"A Safety Plan"

Finding safety and support for the victim of domestic violence requires a plan. According to the New York State Office for the Prevention of Domestic Violence, "Safety planning is the process of evaluating the risks and benefits of different options and identifying ways to reduce the risk."[33] A safety plan will be unique to each individual's situation. As I look back at my experience with Jeffrey, I wish I had been aware of the importance of a safety plan. I was focused on simple moment-by-moment survival most of the time. I was unable to see tomorrow. I know this is the case with many others who find themselves where I was. Even when you are operating in moment-by-moment survival mode and cannot escape, you can implement a safety plan. For example, as Jeffrey moved into stage two of the cycle, which is the abusing incident, I needed to be acutely aware of my surroundings. The living room is the safest place in the house. I could go there. Most rooms of the house hold dangers and possessions that the

---

33 New York State Office for the Prevention of Domestic Violence: www.opdv.state.ny.us

abuser can use in his attack. Taking refuge in the bathroom will leave you cornered and the abuser can use medications and water to sedate and drown their victims. The bedroom provides the abuser with items that can be used for binding and tying his victim, as well as smothering. Guns and other weapons can be hidden in closets. The kitchen provides the abuser with numerous weapons in the form of knives and utensils, as well as cleaning agents and plastic bags. The garage and basement areas provide the abuser with a variety of chemicals, tools and sports equipment that can render his victim helpless as well. Being aware of your surroundings can be part of an immediate safety plan, implemented in the midst of an inescapable crisis. The Domestic Violence Sourcebook notes, "If violence is unavoidable, make yourself a small target; dive into a corner and curl up in a ball with your face protected and arms around each side of your head, fingers entwined."[34] Looking beyond the immediate, into the obscure tomorrow, requires careful thought and planning. Proceed with caution and lay out the safety plan carefully. Consider every option. Remember, this is a plan to be *safe*. Do not take unnecessary risks as you formulate and implement your plan.

---

34 Sandra Judd (editor) Domestic Violence Sourcebook, 4th Edition (Detroit, Michigan: Omnigraphics, Inc., 2013), 472. Used by Permission.

When you are formulating your safety plan, there are several factors to consider. This can be an overwhelming process. Start with simple steps, one at a time, and you will see your plan fall into place. Where will you stay and for how long are you able to stay there? Consider the home of a family member or a close friend, a hotel, or a domestic violence shelter. There are negatives associated with each of these choices and those are things to consider as well. Family members or close friends may not want to become that involved, an extended hotel stay can be costly, and shelters are sometimes so full that they are forced to turn victims away. Regardless of your course of action, keep the contact phone numbers handy and accessible for when you need them. Consider how you will get there. Will you drive, take public transportation, or arrange for a ride from someone you trust? There are also important items that you should plan to take with you. Cash, debit cards, credit cards and a checkbook will be important. Remember that these things on a joint account can be traced or even terminated if they are shared with your abuser. You may need cash for food, lodging, transportation, or even phone calls. Make sure that you know all of your account numbers and passwords. You may want to write them down in a safe place so that you do not have to rely on your memory when you are in a stressed, fight-or-flight state of mind. You will also need identification for yourself as well as your children. This could be your driver's license, birth certificates, social security cards, passports or school ID's. You will need your keys to the house, the car, your office, and perhaps the safe deposit box if you have one. You should have all important paperwork such as medical and immunization records, orders of protection, separation or divorce agreements, custody orders, visitation orders, and child support orders. Make sure that you also have any evidence of abuse with you. This may be in the form of photographs, police reports, medical records, or a journal. Part of your safety plan should be where you could leave extra clothes for yourself and your children, important papers, keys and money. An immediate escape to where these things are will get you on your way to safety.

When you are formulating your safety plan, consider whether you will leave the home or you will have the abuser leave the home. If you plan to stay in the home, consider your continued safety. How will you continue to stay safe there? Consider changing the locks on the doors and the windows. You may need to replace wooden doors with steel or metal doors. You may want to install a security system with additional locks, door bars, or electronic alarms. Fire ladders are a good addition to the second floor as a means of escape out the window. Make sure that you have smoke detectors and fire extinguishers on each floor of the house. When you are formulating your safety plan, include your children. Teach them how to get out of the house and/or how to get help, if necessary. Teach them that it is their job to stay safe, not to stay in harm's way to protect you. If they are old enough and immediate escape is necessary, arrangements could be made in advance for your children to go to a friend's house for safety. If your children are using Facebook or other social media, talk to them about being careful about what they post. Your family can be tracked through this media, which could be dangerous if you have left and are trying to live undetected by your abuser. Make sure that everyone involved in your children's care is made aware of your situation. Make sure they have copies of all legal papers and a photograph of the abuser. This is your responsibility. Without legal papers, they cannot help you.

You may or may not want to get an order of protection. This is a document that may help protect you from harassment or abuse. An order of protection is NOT a guarantee of your safety. According to the New York State Office for the Prevention of Domestic Violence, "In an order of protection, a judge can set limits on your partner's behavior. Among other things, judges in all courts (Criminal, Family and Supreme) can:

- Order your partner to leave and stay away from your home, your workplace, and your family (this is called a "stay away" provision)

- Order your partner to stop abusing you, your children and your pets

- Order your partner to have no contact with you – including no phone calls, letters, emails or messages through other people

Once an order of protection is issued, only a judge can change it. Orders of protection are valid in any state or territory in the country, no matter where they were issued. If the order is not expired and has the correct names of the people involved, the police should consider it valid and enforce it.

Only a small percentage of domestic violence victims seek an order of protection. Violations of these orders are common and often associated with significant danger to the victim. One two-year follow-up study of batterers found that almost one half (48.8%) re-abused the victims after the issuance of the order."[35]

---

[35] New York State Office for the Prevention of Domestic Violence: www.opdv.state.ny.us

Clearly, the choice is yours when it comes to an Order of Protection. While they are immediately available, they are not always effective in protecting you.

Each situation is unique. There are steps in this plan that I would have been unable to take. There are some steps that simply did not apply in my situation. For example, my children were too young to involve them with code words and escape plans. I encourage you to formulate a safety plan that can be implemented when necessary and provide for your ultimate safety. I also encourage you to know the phone number of your local woman's shelter. The shelter will not only provide you with safety and a place to stay, but with valuable resources that will help you reclaim your power and sense of direction. The support services the shelter can provide include individual counseling, support groups, referrals for housing assistance, referrals to transitional housing, food, clothing, crisis intervention and children's programs. This will all take time and you will need to be patient. I would like to note here, that once you are in a safe place, you need to make time to take care of yourself. You may have children with you and yes, they have needs. You have needs too. Give your children all of the attention and care they need, but do not neglect yourself. You have just been through a war and you need to tend to your wounds. Talk with someone, rest when you can, find a creative outlet, read to expand your mind, exercise, dress nicely and put on makeup because it will help you feel better. Make the time to take care of yourself. This will also help you be a better parent and give you strength to fight battles that lie ahead. The fog that obscures your view of tomorrow will lift and the sun will shine in your life again. There is hope. There is life beyond the abuse.

"For I know the plans I have for you," declares the Lord, "plans to prosper you and not to harm you, plans to give you hope and a future." (Jeremiah 29:11)[36]

The Women of Faith Study Bible explains this verse: "God knows the future and wants us to trust Him for the journey ahead. When we feel like abandoned captives, He promises His presence. When we tire of waiting for distant dreams, He promises strength. No matter how bleak our circumstances, God promises "hope and a future".[37]

Hold on to His promise.

---

[36] Women of Faith Study Bible (Grand Rapids, Michigan: Zondervan Corporation, 2001), 1281.

[37] Women of Faith Study Bible (Grand Rapids, Michigan: Zondervan Corporation, 2001), 1281.

Chapter Eleven

"Facing Goliath"

The book of First Samuel Chapter Seventeen in the Bible tells the story about a young boy named David. David was the youngest in his family and he tended the sheep. While he tended the sheep, he honed his skill of using a slingshot to protect the sheep from predators. There came a time when Saul and the Israelites faced a formidable opponent named Goliath. Goliath was a Philistine. He was over nine feet tall and wore a suit of bronze armor. His suit of armor weighed about 127 pounds and the point of his spear alone weighed about 15 pounds. All he had to do was step out and the Israelites ran in fear. David approached Saul and offered to face this giant and kill him. David reminded Saul of the greatness of his God and how God had protected him from so many other dangers. Saul granted David permission to face the giant. In preparation for battle, David tried on a suit of armor. He found it cumbersome because he was not used to wearing it and he took it off. Instead, he armed himself with his slingshot, five smooth stones from a stream, his confidence in his great God and the power of His mighty name. That is all he had and it was clearly all that he needed. This young boy told Goliath that he came in the name of the Lord Almighty. He took a stone from his bag, slung it with his slingshot and hit the giant right in the middle of the forehead and killed him. He overcame a formidable opponent because of his faith.

"Dear brothers and sisters, whenever trouble comes your way, let it be an opportunity for joy. For when your faith is tested, your endurance has a chance to grow. So let it grow, for when your endurance is fully developed, you will be strong in character and ready for anything." (James 1:2-4)[38]

At this time in my life, I felt like the Israelites facing Goliath. I had no self-esteem, no support, no confidence and I was terrified. I did not really know this God that David knew and I certainly did not have the confidence that David had. I faced the formidable challenge of rebuilding our lives and it was intimidating. I knew it would be an arduous task. God does not promise us a problem-free life. He does promise to be with us and give us all that we need to endure. Look at what I had survived! When I considered that, I was somehow reassured that I could rebuild our lives. Yet, the task before me was overwhelming. Here I was, 25 years old, a single mom with two small boys to care for, ages eighteen months and four years old. Where do I

---

38 New Living Translation: www.biblestudytools.com

even begin? I had gone from the shelter of living with my mother, to my marriage to Jeffrey, who took care of everything for me. Sadly, there was plenty I did not know. I had never been taught how to budget money. I did not know how to use a public laundromat or ride a public bus. I had to learn all of these things and more. I did the very best I could at the time. I had no one to show me the way. I sought assistance that was available to us through Social Services such as WIC, food stamps, HEAP, clothing outlets, food banks and Catholic Charities. The Salvation Army granted me temporary shelter in one of their homes and then loaned me money for a security deposit and first month's rent on an apartment. I secured a full time job at a daycare center which my boys could also attend. Life was slowly improving. We were safe and we were basically happy. There was no more violence in our lives.

In spite of my efforts to rebuild our lives, my boys did suffer from the trauma of what we had been through. They both had enormous anxiety and separation issues. Even going to school was a battle. They thought I was going away and never coming back, leaving them in the hands of strangers. The aftermath effects of domestic violence on children have been researched and documented over many years. This research confirms that children who have witnessed domestic violence are affected just as much as if they were being physically abused themselves. Every year, over three million children witness violence in their home. The Alabama Coalition Against Domestic Violence explains the effects on children this way: "Children react to their environment in different ways, and reacting can vary depending on the child's gender and age. Children exposed to family violence are more likely to develop social, emotional, psychological and/or behavioral problems than those who are not. Recent research indicates that children who witness domestic violence show more anxiety, low self-esteem, depression, anger and temperament problems than children who do not witness violence in the home. The trauma they experience can show up in emotional, behavioral, social and physical disturbances that affect their development and can continue into adulthood. Some potential effects are:

Emotional:

- grief for family and personal losses
- shame, guilt and self-blame
- confusion about conflicting feelings toward parents
- fear of abandonment, or expressing emotions, the unknown, or personal injury

- anger
- depression and feelings of helplessness and powerlessness
- embarrassment

Behavioral:

- acting out or withdrawing
- aggressive or passive
- refusing to go to school
- care-taking – acting as a parent substitute
- lying to avoid confrontation
- rigid defenses
- excessive attention-seeking
- bedwetting and nightmares
- out of control behavior
- reduced intellectual competency
- manipulation, dependency, mood swings

Social:

- isolation from friends and relatives
- stormy relationships

- difficulty in trusting, especially adults
- poor anger management and problem solving skills
- excessive social involvement to avoid home
- passivity with peers or bullying
- engaged in exploitative relationships as perpetrator or victim

Physical:

- somatic complaints, headaches and stomachaches
- nervous, anxious, short attention span
- tired and lethargic
- frequently ill
- poor personal hygiene
- regression in development
- high risk play
- self abuse[39]

My precious little boys required a lot of tender loving care through this time. I needed to find every

---

[39] Alabama Coalition Against Domestic Violence: www.acadv.org

way that I could to reassure them that everything was going to be okay. I loved them and took care of them in the best way that I was able to. "Nurturing children from abusive homes can bring healing to their lives. In giving needed care to children, it is important for a parent to reflect these essentials:

- Love and Respect: Acknowledge children's right to have their own feelings, friends, activities and opinions. Promote independence, allow for privacy and respect their feelings for the other parent. Believe in them.

- Provide Emotional Security: Talk and act so children feel safe and comfortable expressing themselves. Be gentle. Be dependable.

- Provide Physical Security: Provide healthy food, safe shelter, and appropriate clothing. Teach personal hygiene and nutrition. Monitor safety. Maintain a family routine. Attend to wounds.

- Provide Discipline: Be consistent, ensure that rules are appropriate to age and development of child. Be clear about limits and expectations. Use discipline to instruct, not to punish.

- Give Time: Participate in your children's lives, in their activities, school, sports, special events, celebrations and friends. Include your children in your activities. Reveal who you are to your children.

- Encourage and Support: Be affirming. Encourage children to follow their interests. Let children disagree with you. Recognize improvement. Teach new skills. Let them make mistakes.

- Give Affection: express verbal and physical affection. Be affectionate when your children are physically or emotionally hurt.

- Care for Yourself: Give yourself personal time. Keep yourself healthy. Maintain friendships. Accept love. "[40]

Time passed and our lives improved. When you least expect a surprise, there it is. My friends introduced me to a young man named Ben. Ben and I began to spend time together and our friendship grew. I had no interest in becoming romantically involved with anyone and Ben felt the same way. We simply enjoyed each other's company. There was something special about him that drew me to his presence. Whatever this was

---

[40] Alabama Coalition Against Domestic Violence: www.acadv.org

he had, I wanted. A simple joy and peace exuded from him. When I finally asked Ben what it was, he told me about Jesus. What I saw was Jesus shining through him. My initial thought was, "Oh boy, I've heard about these born-again Christians. I'm not sure about this." My second thought was, "Wow. I really want the joy and peace that he has." A few weeks later, Ben invited me to go to church. I gratefully accepted. My heartstrings were being pulled throughout the service that day as the pastor's message settled into the deepest recesses of my heart. I had known even in my darkest moments that God loved me. I had witnessed firsthand how He had saved me from my imprisoned life. On that beautiful sunny Sunday morning in June, the pastor gave an altar call. As the sun shone through the stained glass windows of the church, God waited at the altar and held His arms open to me. From the last pew at the back of the church, I _ran_ to His open arms.

Until that day, I had experienced God within the confines and teachings of the Catholic Church. I had uttered monotone prayers in unison with the church body, experienced the Sacraments, and followed all of the laws of my Catholic upbringing. God was a faraway and distant entity who watched over the world with judgment. He was the Creator of heaven and earth, God Almighty. Even the Bible was a sacred book that only the priest could touch.

That beautiful, sunny June day opened the door for me to experience God in a personal and intimate way. My eyes were opened to see all that He was, is, and will always be: my Lord and Savior. As I began to learn about this personal and loving God, I was able to see all that He had done for me. Jesus gave His life for me. He died in my place so that I could enjoy the freedom of salvation and live life abundantly. As I reflected back at my life and all that I had experienced up to that point, I was awestruck. He healed me from a near fatal illness; He protected me from my father's abuse; He prevented a pregnancy from my rape; and He saved me and my precious little boys from imprisonment and abuse. Almost instantly, I recognized this great God as a physician and healer, as well as a great protector. Ultimately, He was my stronghold, my place of survival and refuge. As time passed, I would come to know Him as so much more. The journey held so much promise and hope for me. God had so much more to show me and to teach me.

    Jeffrey was still present in our lives, as he had visitation with the boys. He continued to harass and intimidate me. I was completely unaware that statistics show that the most dangerous time for a victim of domestic violence is actually *after* she leaves. I stood my ground. I knew we were better off without him, even though it was difficult to make ends meet. As time went on, the visitation became inconsistent. Sometimes he would simply not show up. The child support checks became sparse and eventually stopped coming completely. With the assistance of my attorney, I presented Jeffrey with an opportunity to stop supporting his children. He seized that opportunity. In exchange of paying thousands of dollars in arrear support or paying any support in the future, he gave up his parental rights completely. In 1989, I made one of the best decisions of my life. After years of severe mental, emotional and physical abuse, I stood up to my abuser. He walked away. I was finally *completely free.*

Chapter Twelve

"Moving Forward"

Our lives had once again become normal. "Family" consisted of the three of us. My family all lived geographically far away and Jeffrey's family was no longer a part of our lives. We were surrounded by supportive friends and a church family. I had found a better job in the field of Early Childhood Education and a generous friend had given me a car.

I was at work one day when a dad came in to pick up his son. His son attended morning Kindergarten and came to the daycare center for the afternoon until it was time to go home. Philip had visitation and it was his day to pick up his son. We shared conversation on that day and each day after that when he came in. After six months, Philip asked me out. We dated for a year. He was carefree and charming. While we were camping one weekend, Philip proposed. He wanted to share his life with me and my boys. I delightfully accepted.

As Philip and I moved forward with our wedding plans, we received opposition from my friends and his family. Neither one of us could understand this opposition. My friends insisted that this union would not be a positive one. I did not feel that my friends had spent enough time with Philip to know him. Philip's family expressed extreme opposition to our marriage for reasons unknown to me. His mother was the most outspoken. On the evening of our wedding rehearsal, she told Philip, in my presence, that he was making the biggest mistake of his life. Philip chose to ignore his family and marry me in spite of their objections.

Six weeks after our wedding, I became very ill. I had flu-like symptoms and extreme fatigue. At first, I made attempts to continue life as usual, but the fatigue took me over. I began to fall asleep at work and even fall asleep at stoplights in my car. I could not stay awake no matter how hard I tried. Soon, I was incapacitated by whatever this illness was. I slept 20 hours a day for six weeks. Our neighbors and Philip's family began to help care for the boys. I began to see my doctor twice a week. Philip would wake me, dress me, and get me in the car. I would sleep on the drive there and he would wake me to go inside. I would sleep in the waiting room, sleep in the exam room while waiting for the doctor, and sleep on the ride home. My doctor performed test after test, seeking a diagnosis by eliminating what diseases it was not. One day, I was in her office receiving IV fluids. My blood pressure had dropped dangerously low. She looked at me and said, "You should be dead. I…don't know…what's wrong." I slept for several hours in her office that day, while receiving those IV fluids. My blood pressure began to rise and she released me to go home. Slowly, ever so slowly, I began to recover. Each day, I gained a little more strength. I was able to stay awake for longer periods of time. I was still limited with my activity. Weeks passed and my doctor was finally able to reach the diagnosis of Chronic Fatigue Syndrome. As I began to get stronger, she warned me. "You could get this sick again. Next time, it may not be as bad, or it could be worse," she said. "I will never be this sick again." I professed adamantly. Three months later, I was strong enough to lift a laundry basket. A month after that, I could carry bags of groceries. Life began to return to normal. God was my healer and protector.

After that, life with Philip was wonderful. He adopted my boys and we felt like one family. We were always busy and our lives were full of activity. We became avid campers. Each Friday we would pack up and head off for another weekend camping adventure. All three boys were doing well in school. All three boys were involved in sports – soccer, baseball and football. I discovered a wonderful church and established myself in ministry there. Philip and I added to our family and had two beautiful daughters. They brought so much joy to our lives! The boys doted over the girls, watched over them and protected them. As the girls grew, they became involved in activities as well: chorus, dance, marching band colorguard and winterguard. I became an employee of the church as director of their preschool. Our lives were busy with work and raising five children.

There came another occasion in my life when I was reminded of Psalm 91. Philip and I were driving in our van to pick up our son. We approached an intersection that had a reputation for being dangerous. Although we had a green light, we approached the intersection with caution. Philip asked me to double check that there was no traffic coming from the other direction. I looked out the window, saw no traffic at all, and told him to go ahead. I looked out my window again as we were turning left. The only thing I could see was the letters MACK only inches from my window. I do not know where that semi had come from. There was no sound of a horn; there were no squealing brakes from the truck. "For He will command His angels concerning you to guard you in all your ways; they will lift you up in their hands so that you will not strike your foot against a stone." (Psalm 91:11-12)[41]

---

[41] Women of Faith Study Bible (Grand Rapids, Michigan: Zondervan Corporation, 2001), 956.

I believe *without a doubt* that God's angels stood between that truck and our van to protect me. I have no other explanation as to why that semi never touched our van. Philip kept driving, completely unaware of what had just happened. I, on the other hand, had just witnessed God's hand of protection once again. I looked in the side view mirror to see the truck pull over to the shoulder of the road. I can only imagine the thoughts of that truck driver as he tried to grasp the intensity of what had just happened.

After ten years of marriage, the beautiful tapestry of our lives began to unravel. Philip's mother was diagnosed with lung cancer and passed away. Her death affected him deeply. I could certainly empathize. Only eighteen months later, Philip's father passed away. He would never be the same. Philip became extremely depressed and started to drink excessively. He often isolated himself from the family. Philip would live in the bedroom, spending time on the computer, watching TV, and even eating his meals in there. He began to do everything for himself. He would cook meals for himself. He would buy groceries for himself. His relationships with everyone began to suffer. Philip was an embarrassment to our children. They stopped asking friends to come over. Needless to say, our marriage also suffered the consequences of his alcoholism. I found myself in a state of disbelief, questioning how I could possibly be in this position again. I was not subject to physical abuse as I had been in my previous marriage. The abuse I suffered with Philip was emotional and psychological. While the abuse was not always obvious to our children, I knew that they were suffering as well. My marriage to Philip left all of us suffering from years of emotional abuse and neglect.

Chapter Thirteen

"Secret Places of My Heart"

Throughout those years, my greatest outlet for my emotions was my journal. The pages of my journal helped me to maintain an ongoing record of events as well as serve as an outlet for all that I was feeling in the secret spaces of my heart. For years I filled the pages of my journal with my triumphs and joys, my heartaches and sorrows. My journal became an integral part of my journey.

Journaling is an ancient tradition that dates back as far as 10th century Japan. Many successful people journal as a part of their everyday lives. I have found journaling to be a wonderful release for my feelings. I have gained perspective and a better understanding of myself and my life.

In an article written for Psychology Today, Jordan Gaines Lewis writes, "In a 2004 study published in <u>Psychological Science,</u> Pennebaker and colleagues were among the first researchers to explore the power of written expression during psychological distress using a similar mass-blogging data analysis. The researchers downloaded Live Journal entries of 1,084 public blogs for four months – two months prior to and two months after the September 11 attacks. This method also allowed them to collect age, gender and location information based on information from their public profiles. Using the text analysis program Linguistic Inquiry and Word Count (LIWC), each word in the 78,000 entries was checked against a dictionary of 2,300 words and characterized by four basic categories: emotional positivity, cognitive processing, social orientation, and psychological distancing.

Pennebaker found that shortly after the 9/11 attacks (less than two weeks), the blogs expressed significantly more negative emotions and were written with greater psychological distancing. After two weeks, the writers' "moods" returned to baseline (two months before the attacks), but psychological distancing remained elevated over six weeks. Although all effects were stronger for individuals highly preoccupied with 9/11 (i.e., those shown to blatantly write about the events more often), comparable language changes were seen overall.

Although this analysis method is still relatively new and flawed, it shows promise to real-time tracking of response to drastic changes as they naturally unfold, providing a continuous timeline on a massive and diverse scale. This study in particular demonstrates the ability for humans to affiliate more during periods of threat as well as a –

perhaps unconscious – concern of individual victims, their community, and/or the entire nation. While zero entries revealed writers' feelings of involvement with a large social group (such as a city or country) before the attacks, 44% of post-9/11 entries did."[42]

Journaling can be a powerful tool. There have been many other benefits of journaling recorded. Appleseeds.org presents a list of 100 Benefits of Journaling.[43]

Here is a small sampling of some of my entries from my life with Philip:

August 17, 1998: The emotional abuse continues. Little notes everywhere, like I am a child. Constant digs all day long. I just want to stop hurting.

July 25, 1999: Philip is still drinking, sitting at that damn computer. He stopped working on the house, stopped all of his "projects". But in the process, it's as though he has stopped caring. About anything.

September 7, 1999: I wrote Philip a really nice letter about my love for him. He wouldn't read it –

---

[42] Jordan Gaines Turning Trauma into Story: The Benefits of Journaling, Psychology Today, www.psychologytoday.com
[43] 100 Benefits of Journaling www.appleseeds.org

just threw it aside. He got up early the next morning and wrote me back. A really nasty letter. It crushed my spirit. I sat for a long time at my vanity, feeling that suicide was the only answer, the only way out of my pain. I'll never be the same. My heart is just broken. Everything I am was torn apart in that letter – wife, mother, teacher, Christian. The inside of me feels so completely and totally crushed.

December 25, 1999: Philip was passed out when it was time for church. Passed out when it was time to be "Santa". Passed out when it was time to open gifts. Passed out when it was time for dinner. When he *was* up and moving, he was stumbling, slurring, tripping and falling into the Christmas tree. Merry Christmas.

December 26, 1999: The furnace has stopped. Philip left me a note to buy us a new furnace, got drunk and went to bed. "Not my problem", he wrote.

January 5, 2000: I was feeling cold and he had the furnace turned down to 65 degrees. I put on another layer of clothes and I turned the furnace up to 67 degrees. When Philip discovered that I had turned the furnace up, he turned it back down and said, "If you ever touch that thermostat again, I will break both of your arms."

August 23, 2000: I feel so shut out of his life. He doesn't share his thoughts or feelings. He talks about the weather and sometimes his job. That's it.

January 10, 2001: My heart is so broken over my marriage and my home life here. I have been pouring my heart into the pages of this journal for so long. Nothing changes. Philip's heart has hardened. He is so different now. So closed off and so far away. There is so much space. So much emptiness. So much pain and hurt. When will it ever end?

August 3, 2002: I do everything alone. Everything in my life – work, school events, church events, social events. I am always alone and I hate it. Philip used to be such a socialite. Now he's a hermit. He is never with me. I do everything alone.

December 25, 2002: I do not begin to understand Philip. He was completely closed off and distant today...more than ever. He didn't say much of anything to anyone. He stayed in his room. When we ate, he wouldn't eat with us. When the kids were here, he stayed away. Merry Christmas. I just don't understand why he chooses to live this way.

April 30, 2003: I saw the TMJ doctor today for a consult. My headaches and ear pain are from my jaw joint. It goes back to when Jeffrey threw me against the wall. The doctor says the jaw joint was never properly treated after that trauma. It will cost me about $3000 to fix it. How unfair that all this time later I have to suffer so much for what he did to me.

September 24, 2003: My marriage remains absolutely the same. No change at all. In spite of my conviction and my commitment to resolve our issues, Philip continues to reject me and put me off.

October 6, 2003: In discussing upcoming expenses with Philip, he told me, "You're already working two jobs. Get another one."

October 9, 2003: I have asked Philip to make time for me so we can talk and he refuses.

October 12, 2003: I tried to explain to Philip that the waterbed must have a small leak because I am waking up wet in the morning. He insisted there is no leak and that I must be wetting the bed.

October 20, 2003: It's been a week since I moved out of the bedroom. I am sleeping upstairs. He is not going to pay for the newspaper or the phone anymore. This is becoming strangely reminiscent of my last month with Jeffrey.

November 3, 2003: Philip cut off the internet with no explanation. I can't stand that he makes decisions that affect the whole family and he cares nothing about the fallout. I am not affected by this decision as much as the kids are. They will have to go to the library to use the computer. That's six miles away.

November 7, 2003: I have smelled something really awful in the house for a couple of days now. Like something died. I began to search, almost frantically, to find the source of the smell, only to find that Philip unplugged the upright freezer and did not tell anyone. We had about $300 worth of meat in there, amongst other things. I found the source of that smell was all of that meat spoiling and rotting. I simply do not understand what he is doing or why he is doing all of this.

November 26, 2003: This week he fixed my van instead of buying groceries. There is no money to buy food.

February 11, 2004: Because he is always on his computer, I wrote an email to Philip. I want him to talk with me and deal with our issues. I found out that he has me blocked and will not accept my emails. That speaks volumes to me...

February 16, 2004: He gave me chocolate covered cherries for Valentine's Day. We have been together for 18 years. I HATE chocolate covered cherries. I always have.

June 2, 2004: This whole house smells like alcohol. You can smell it as soon as you walk in the front door. There is almost nowhere you can go to escape it. It is disgusting. Philip is so oblivious.

June 21, 2004: Father's Day was yesterday. Philip was an ass. He would not even get out of the car when the kids and I took him out to dinner.

September 6, 2004: Philip's drinking is really out of control. He can't even walk straight most of the time.

December 12, 2004: My son confronted Philip about his drinking and his so-called life. He closed both of them in the bedroom. My son was yelling at him and he even punched a hole in my bedroom wall. I don't know if it will really make a difference or not. Philip hasn't hit bottom. So, as usual, Philip stayed up all night, drinking and on the computer. He crawled into bed when I got up to start my day. And again… nothing changes…except now, there's a hole in the wall.

December 26, 2004: Christmas is over. It was a lousy one for me. Philip got me a box of chocolates and lounging pajamas size 2X. I am a size 6.

January 11, 2005: An uneventful birthday. My pizza dinner this year was English muffin pizzas. Yippee. My card from Philip was a piece of paper that said, "Happy Birthday, Karen (my last name). Love, Philip". Nothing else.

January 31, 2005: I need to talk to Philip. Real changes need to happen. Then I will make decisions. The funny thing is, in spite of it all, I love him. I really want to make things work. I've shared my life with this man for 20 years. Things could be so different if we just worked at it.

October 18, 2005: I really did not think it would be possible for Philip to isolate himself from us any more than he already has. Yet, he has found a way. He barely talks to any of us anymore. Like we are not even here.

October 30, 2005: I feel as though I don't even know this man anymore. Last week, he told me that if he had been in charge of FEMA, he never would have sent any help at all to New Orleans after hurricane Katrina hit because they were so stupid to build their city the way they did. That statement struck me so hard! What a heartless thing to say. What happened to the loving, sensitive and charming man I married almost 20 years ago?

Chapter Fourteen

"Discovery"

Why tolerate the abuse? Why didn't I just leave? This time I viewed my situation differently. My life was not in danger. The bottom line was that I was willing to do whatever it took to fix the marriage. I was not willing to walk away until I knew in my heart that I had done everything to fix it. I was aware of research that indicated a Christian woman was more inclined to stay in an abusive relationship because she did not want to disappoint God. I was a Christian woman and I felt it was my duty to stay and fix it. I opened God's Word to search for my answers.

"You ask 'Why?' It is because the Lord is acting as the witness between you and the wife of your youth, because you have broken faith with her, though she is your partner, the wife of your marriage covenant. Has not the Lord made them one? In flesh and spirit they are his. And why one? Because he was seeking godly offspring. So guard yourself in your spirit, and do not break faith with the wife of your youth. 'I hate divorce,' says the Lord God of Israel, 'and I hate a man's covering himself with violence as well as with his garment,' says the Lord Almighty. 'So guard yourself in your spirit, and do not break faith.' (Malachi 2:14-16)[44]

The Women of Faith Bible explains this Scripture this way, "The men of Judah are smashing into bits God's ideal of marriage. They are divorcing their wives to marry pagan women. While this passage depicts such behavior as unfaithfulness to the original wives and to God, the verses also remind us of God's ideal for marriage. It is God's design that both partners strive to keep their promise to be faithful and that each endeavors to become one with the other in "flesh and spirit" (Mal. 2:15), signifying their physical and spiritual intimacy. Out of this union, God wants "godly offspring" (Mal. 2:15) – both the children who are born to the couple and the couple themselves are God's offspring.(Acts 17:28-29). As God's and as godly, they are inclined toward a strong relationship with the Lord. The passage closes with a statement of how damaging divorce is to the spirit. Regardless of how justifiable the reasons for divorce may seem, divorce does violence to everyone involved.[45]

---

[44] Women of Faith Study Bible (Grand Rapids, Michigan: Zondervan Corporation, 2001), 1573-1574.

[45] Women of Faith Study Bible (Grand Rapids, Michigan: Zondervan Corporation, 2001), 1574.

I was so touched by what I was reading, I decided to look up the exact meanings of the words "strive" and "endeavor". To strive means "to exert much effort or energy; to struggle or fight forcefully"[46] To endeavor means to "make a conscientious or concerted effort toward an end; an earnest attempt"[47] I realized at that moment that I had not done everything I needed to do. I did not strive nor did I endeavor to make changes. I also needed to discover my part in the problem. I had to be accountable for my behavior. This would take some serious soul-searching. I immersed myself in a number of books that began to put me on a path of self discovery.

In "The Power of a Praying Wife", Stormie Omartian's words reached into the depths of my heart. "The power that resurrected Jesus is the very same power that will resurrect the dead places of your marriage and put life back into it. But it doesn't happen without a heart for God that is willing to gut it out in prayer, grow through tough times, and wait for love to be resurrected. We have to go through the pain to get to the joy. You have to decide if you want your marriage to work, and if you want it badly enough to do whatever is necessary, within healthy parameters, to see it

---

46 www.thefreedictionary.com

47 www.thefreedictionary.com

happen."[48] I certainly had a heart for God. I was praying. I was in pain, just waiting for the joy. I wanted this marriage to work. The words "healthy parameters" struck me. Nothing about this marriage resided in healthy parameters.

Around this time, some friends and I attended a women's conference at a local church. The words of the keynote speaker touched my heart. Here is what she said: "Detach. Take your heart out of the situation and do what you are supposed to do. Fulfill your role. Pray for God to change *you*." Fully realizing that I could not change Philip, I prayed for God to change me. I prayed that I could search within myself to find the answers that I needed and that God would reveal His purposes to me.

My campaign to search myself included reading numerous books. "God Will Make a Way" by Henry Cloud and John Townsend confirmed my direction. "If your spouse has chosen to disconnect from your marriage, understand that God's way does not include changing your spouse unless your spouse invites Him to do so. Follow God and His ways, no matter what your spouse chooses to do. God's way for you is always that you become the most

---

48 Stormie Omartian The Power of a Praying Wife (Eugene, Oregon: Harvest House Publishers, 1997), 20. Used by Permission.

healthy, loving, holy and righteous person you can be. That is your part." [49]

Over the years, I sought counsel with three pastors associated with my church. Each session provided me with new perspective and new insights. I faithfully applied everything as I was counseled by my pastors. Nothing changed within the context of my marriage. Dr. John Townsend writes, "One of the most powerful principles that helps people begin to see changes in their relationship involves retrieving, recapturing and reclaiming control over their own happiness, which they have shifted to their button-pusher. It is very easy to feel that unless your person changes, you are bereft of love, or frustrated, powerless or unhappy. That is, the person holds the golden key to a major part of your life, and as long as he does not cooperate, your life suffers significantly."[50]

I *was* suffering, even though I was busy and involved with working and ministry work at the church; and I was involved in the children's lives and their activities. At the urging of my pastor, I sought counseling through a local Christian

---

[49] Henry Cloud, Dr. John Townsend God Will Make a Way: What to Do When You Don't Know What to Do (Brentwood, Tennessee: Integrity Publishers, 2002), 130-131.

[50] Dr. John Townsend Who's Pushing Your Buttons? (Brentwood, Tennessee: Integrity Publishers, 2004), 80.

counseling organization. I attended my sessions faithfully every week for eighteen months. The personal growth and healing that took place during those eighteen months was phenomenal. I searched my soul, sought God's direction, and found healing for my broken heart. The emotional intensity of those eighteen months cannot be underestimated. There were times that I did not feel I could continue the excruciating task of healing. The work of recovery and healing is a long and difficult process. I pushed through because I knew without a doubt that I would be a better person because of it. I came to terms with my feelings about my father. With the guidance of my counselor, I went under hypnosis and re-lived my rape with Kyle. I was able to face my demons from my marriage to Jeffrey. I could clearly observe patterns of behavior within myself in the context of each of these relationships in my life. Each week, my counselor gave me a homework assignment. These assignments took considerable effort to complete. Many homework assignments included frank discussions with Philip concerning difficult issues we struggled with during our marriage. Philip's complacency often made my assignments unbearable. I persevered. At the end of my eighteen month personal journey, I found myself. I was equipped with a better understanding of the events in my life and how the patterns of my relationships affected my decisions. The only thing that was still eluding me was forgiveness. I still needed to forgive the abusers in my life. I needed to forgive myself for mistakes I had made. I still had work to do. Forgiveness would come much later.

One of the books I was reading was "Loving God with All Your Mind" by Elizabeth George. I was profoundly affected by her written words, especially when I read this, "I was forced to face reality. You see, because of my unmet expectations I was postponing any action. Because I didn't like what I saw (which was real!), I was failing to do anything to try to improve the situation. I neglected to deal with the circumstances. Furthermore, I wasn't prepared to because "this wasn't the way it was supposed to be!" And as long as I had that attitude - as long as I didn't accept reality – no progress or solution was possible. As long as I wished for reality to be different, I failed to handle the problem, which was quite real! You see, once we accept reality – the reality of the condition of our marriage, our family, our job, whatever – we can then use our time and energy to make that reality better."[51] I was there in every way. I cannot tell you how many times I screamed out, "This isn't the way it was supposed to be!" This marriage was supposed to be different. This marriage was supposed to be

---

51 Elizabeth George Loving God With All Your Mind (Eugene, Oregon: Harvest House Publishers, 1994/2005), 60. Used by Permission.

"happily ever after". Reading these words so eloquently penned by Elizabeth George pushed me towards facing and accepting the reality of my marriage.

Dr. Townsend also wrote, "Denial can rob you of life and years; so it is worth it to work through it and see reality as it is. Reality is always your friend."[52]

Until that point, my denial had definitely robbed me of years. I had done all of the hard work that was necessary. Only then could I clearly see that over the years I had done everything that I possibly could to save my marriage. I knew in my heart that I had done all that I could do. Reality was staring me in the face and it was time to let go. After 22 years with Philip, we ended our marriage with a divorce.

---

52 Dr. John Townsend Who's Pushing Your Buttons? (Brentwood, Tennessee: Integrity Publishers, 2004), 53.

Chapter Fifteen

"Forgiveness"

The divorce was emotionally draining. Philip was angry and verbally abusive. He manipulated and undermined my efforts to make everything equal. Ultimately, he felt I was entitled to nothing from our 22 years together and manipulated the system to believe him. At the end of the proceedings, I was left holding my broken heart and not much else. I was shaken to find myself in this place yet again. I thought we would be together forever. Still, as I reflected on the situation in the silence of my new apartment, I knew that I could move on. I had endured so much worse. This time, I was stronger and in a better position to deal with everything that came my way. I had a good job, steady income, a church family, and my children were grown. Most importantly, I had my relationship with Jesus. All of this would make an enormous difference for me.

Just after I left Philip, I went to the doctor for a routine checkup. The day after my appointment, I received a phone call from my doctor's nurse. Routine tests that had been performed the previous day revealed a concern with my heart valve. I had always had a heart murmur, but the doctor was particularly concerned about what she saw in the test results and immediately referred me to a cardiologist. I had the appointment with the cardiologist within a few days, and I walked out of his office in shock. He determined that I was in Stage A heart failure. I had a crazy amount of different thoughts running through my head as I tried to process all of the information that he had told me. "Why now?" I asked myself. The only answer that I could come up with was that Philip had truly broken my heart. I called my best friend on the phone and shared everything with her. After a lengthy discussion, she completely agreed with me that the divorce from Philip had broken my heart.

Moving forward, I set my sights on healing and self-care. I carefully followed dietary restrictions set by my doctor and began a daily exercise routine. I continued to journal, pray, and attend church regularly. When I spent time silently reflecting on my journey, I could always see God's hand gently guiding me forward. In my times of quiet reassessment, I discovered that I was angry and unforgiving about the way that Philip had treated me and our children, especially our daughters. I also remembered that my anger and unforgiveness went back a long way in my life, to Jeffrey, Kyle and my father. I knew that the only way to be free was to forgive them. This seemed an almost impossible task, yet I knew God's promise in Luke 1:37, "Nothing is impossible with God."[53] There are countless stories in the Bible of people who faced insurmountable odds and experienced in their humanity what appeared to be impossible. Yet God used those experiences to prove that His promise stands true, that nothing is impossible if you believe in Him. I began the task of working my way to forgiveness. Where do I begin? I always begin with God and His Word.

"I will instruct you and teach you in the way you should go; I will counsel you and watch over you." (Psalm 32:8)[54]

"Trust in the Lord with all your heart and lean not on your own understanding; in all your ways acknowledge Him, and He will make your paths straight." (Prov.3:5-6)[55]

In their book, "God Will Make A Way", Dr. Henry Cloud and Dr. John Townsend share these thoughts on forgiveness:

---

53 Women of Faith Study Bible (Grand Rapids, Michigan: Zondervan Corporation, 2001), 1680

54 Women of Faith Study Bible (Grand Rapids, Michigan: Zondervan Corporation, 2001), 887.

55 Women of Faith Study Bible (Grand Rapids, Michigan: Zondervan Corporation, 2001), 1021.

"To forgive does not mean that we deny that someone has hurt us. Nor does it mean that we have to necessarily trust them again or allow them into our heart again."

"It's about letting go of what has already happened. It's about acknowledging the things that were done to us and the debt that we are owed."

"As long as we feel like someone "owes us", we're tied to him or her by the offense committed. That's why the Bible uses the word "forgive" which means "to cancel a debt". When we forgive, we are saying the person no longer owes us, and we are releasing that person. Once we have forgiven, the debt is over, and we no longer feel obligated to punish the person or to retaliate."[56]

My personal assessment began to unfold. Yes, they hurt me. Yes, I did not have to let them into my heart again. What happened was over, it could not be changed. My struggle was in the fact that I felt that they owed me and needed to make it right. Forgiveness is a deliberate decision to let go and move on. I wanted and needed to do that, so I began to explore this issue of forgiveness.

---

56 Henry Cloud, Dr. John Townsend God Will Make a Way: What to Do When You Don't Know What to Do (Brentwood, Tennessee: Integrity Publishers, 2002), 54.

Eileen Borris, author of "Finding Forgiveness", lists "Eight Things to Remember About Forgiveness":

- Only we can decide in our own minds and hearts to forgive. In this sense, we are never required to forgive. Forgiveness is perhaps the most generous gesture we can make, not only to those who have wronged us, but to ourselves as well.

- Forgiveness is a state of mind. In this very sense, forgiveness is forgetting. In doing so, we relieve our memories of the burden of revisiting the wound itself and thus reduce our pain.

- Forgiveness is not excusing a wrongdoer. When someone injures us we are *not* required to make believe the wrong did not take place. Forgiveness is deciding to *not* continue to try and collect the debt of the wrong. If someone owes us money and we forgive the debt, we do not participate in the fiction that the money isn't owed. By forgiving the debt, we mean that we are no longer going to waste our precious energies in a futile act. This is important when the debt is really uncollectible, for example, when there has been a wrongful death.

- Forgiveness is reflexive. When we forgive someone who has wronged us, or we forgive the wrong itself, we also benefit from the relief of no longer having to deal with it. We have all known someone who would not forget that he or she was rejected by a lover or by a divorced parent. Often that someone lives his or her whole life making decisions that are colored by the emotional scars left after the perceived wound. This is tantamount to carrying a burden as heavy as the guilt of having committed the wrong in the first place. Often, it is heavier . It is usually wiser to relieve oneself of that burden by forgiving the wrong.

- Forgiveness is liberating. When we are finally able to make the decision to forgive, we feel a lightness as the burden of anger is dropped from our shoulders. Try it. The feeling is almost exhilarating.

- Forgiveness does not equate with loving enemies. No one is ever required to love an enemy. But obsessive hatred costs energy, and, when we nurse a hatred, it is both time- and energy-consuming.

Even in war, it is usually more practical to forgive enemies than to nurse the hatred felt during the war. The disastrous consequences of the harsh Treaty of Versailles after World War I proved that it would have been better for the Allies to extend a hand to Germany rather than punish it for making war. Many historians agree if that help had been extended, Hitler would never have gained a foothold.

- *Forgiveness is never easy, but its efforts are rewarding. Because forgiveness is a matter of mind more than anything else, it requires understanding. The process of this journey of understanding is not to force ourselves to believe that the debt of wrong is not owed, but that to continue to try and collect the debt would cost us more than simply excusing it.

- Forgiveness is self-empowering. It would be easy to assume that forgiving is an act of weakness. In so assuming, we credit those who have wronged us with power, while disempowering ourselves. But forgiving is an act of strength. Remember that when we are wronged, *only we* can forgive the wrongdoer. We possess tremendous power in that respect. By exercising that power we add to it, and, thus proving we have it, we bulk up our self-esteem in the process.[57]

There were many days that I began to feel as though I were moving forward through this forgiveness issue and making progress. Suddenly, I would have contact with Philip and something would be said that would hurt me all over again. There I was, picking up the pieces, crying, angry and hurt yet again. One step forward, two steps back. The unforgiveness that I felt was simply ugly. I discovered that unforgiveness is full of negative emotions like anger, resentment, hostility, vengeance and stress. They are heavy emotions and they weigh you down like a heavy ball and chain around your body. I felt that. I also knew without a doubt that this unforgiveness I felt in my heart was affecting my health. I made the decision that I had to be free of that weight. I needed the freedom to fly and move on with my life.

I began to search the Scriptures to see what God has to say about forgiveness. There are countless Scriptures on this topic. Here are a few that particularly pointed me in the right direction:

---

[57] Eileen R. Borris-Dunchunstang, Ed.D Finding Forgiveness (New York, New York: McGraw Hill Companies, 2007), 53-54. Used by Permission.

"For if you forgive men when they sin against you, your heavenly Father will also forgive you. But if you do not forgive men their sins, your Father will not forgive your sins." (Matthew 6:14,15)[58]

"And when you assume the posture of prayer, remember that it's not all asking. If you have anything against anyone, forgive - only then will your heavenly Father be inclined to also wipe your slate clean of sins." (Mark 11:25)[59]

"Bear with each other and forgive whatever grievances you may have against one another. Forgive as the Lord forgave you." (Colossians 3:13)[60]

    One of my favorites on the topic of forgiveness is the Parable of the Unmerciful Servant, as told by Jesus in Matthew 18:21-35. The study notes of the Women of Faith Study Bible explain this Parable in this way, "So begins one of Jesus' most poignant instructions regarding forgiveness. When Peter asks Jesus how many times he should forgive, Peter is being generous with his suggestion of seven times. Traditional Rabbinic teaching required that an offended person only forgive an offender

---

[58] Women of Faith Study Bible (Grand Rapids, Michigan: Zondervan Corporation, 2001), 1589.
[59] The Message translation: www.biblestudytools.com
[60] Women of Faith Study Bible (Grand Rapids, Michigan: Zondervan Corporation, 2001), 1952.

three times. Jesus answers with hyperbole, essentially saying that no limits on forgiveness apply when we consider the depth and extent to which we have been forgiven by God. Each of us is like the first servant in Jesus' parable whose debt before God is so large – and forgiven – that we have no grounds for withholding forgiveness from anyone."[61]

My ultimate favorite is simply the example set by Jesus himself. Jesus forgave those who were closest to him…Peter for denying him and Judas for betraying him. Even on the cross, "Jesus said, "Father, forgive them, for they do not know what they are doing." (Luke 23:34)[62]

I think if I were searching for the perfect example, I found it. When I looked back at the events of my life and the people that I held responsible, I remembered the words of Jesus on the cross, *"For they do not know what they are doing."* I took those very words and applied them to my life situations. In the case of my father, I was not the subject of his abuse, but I was a witness of it and suffered because of it. He began a legacy of abuse in my life. *"He did not know what he was*

---

[61] Women of Faith Study Bible (Grand Rapids, Michigan: Zondervan Corporation, 2001), 1615.
[62] Women of Faith Study Bible (Grand Rapids, Michigan: Zondervan Corporation, 2001), 1735.

doing." When it came to Kyle, he may have thought he knew what he was doing, in the moment, as he carried out his plan. The long-term effects for me from that fateful day were far from his mind. *"He did not know what he was doing."* Even Kyle's friends, as they chose to help him carry out his plan, did not realize the long term implications of their actions. *"They did not know what they were doing."* My severe and almost life-ending abuse from Jeffrey was next on my mind as I pushed through this topic of forgiveness. He may have thought about his power and control, his drinking, or even his next plan for my abuse, but he was not thinking of how his abuse affected me and our sons for many years to come. *"He did not know what he was doing."* Lastly, my divorce from Philip and the emotional hurt, which was still so fresh and new, needed the same touch of forgiveness as the other situations. I looked at those years and the emotional toll it had taken. I don't believe that either of us had planned for our marriage to take the path it had taken. We had grown apart and allowed our emotions to get the best of us at times. Because of his own deep personal pain, Philip did things and said things to me and our children that hurt deeply. *"He did not know what he was doing."*

I began to see light at the end of this tunnel, so to speak. I could physically feel the weight of this burden of unforgiveness begin to lighten. One evening I read something that profoundly struck me and propelled me forward as though I were on a springboard.

"The Bible is clear about two principles: 1. We always need to forgive, but 2. We don't always achieve reconciliation. Forgiveness is something that we do in our hearts; we release someone from a debt that they owe us. We write off the person's debt, and he no longer owes us. We no longer condemn him. He is clean. Only one party is needed for forgiveness: me. The person who owes me a debt does not have to ask my forgiveness. It is a work of grace in my heart. This brings us to the second principle: we do not always achieve reconciliation. God forgave the world, but the whole world is not reconciled to Him. Although He may have forgiven all people, all people have not owned their sin and appropriated His forgiveness. Forgiveness takes one; reconciliation takes two. We do not open ourselves up to the other party until we have seen that he has truly owned his part of the problem. So many times Scripture talks about keeping boundaries with someone until he owns what he has done and produces "fruit in keeping with repentance." True repentance is much more than saying "I'm sorry"; it is changing direction. Remember, God is your model. He did not wait for people to change their behavior before He stopped condemning them. He is finished condemning, but that does not mean that He has a relationship with all people. People must choose to own up to their sin and repent, then God will open Himself to them. Reconciliation involves two. Do not think that because you have forgiven that you have to reconcile. You can offer reconciliation, but it must not be contingent upon the other person owning his behavior and bringing forth trustworthy fruits."[63]

Reading this was an enormous eye-opener for me. I realized that I had been expecting reconciliation all along. I expected my father to apologize to me. I expected Kyle to apologize to me. I expected Kyle's friends to apologize to me. I expected Jeffrey to apologize to me. I expected Philip to apologize to me. Suddenly I realized that none of them would ever apologize, nor would they ever own up to their actions. I realized how unrealistic my expectations were. Once I came to terms with that, I let go of the unrealistic expectations and made the conscious choice to forgive each of them. I cancelled their debt. They owed me nothing. *They did not know what they were doing.* I found an unspeakable freedom in that decision to release all of it.

---

[63] Henry Cloud, Dr. John Townsend Boundaries: When to Say Yes, How to Say No, to Take Control of Your Life (Grand Rapids, Michigan: Zondervan Corporation, 1992), 257.

Michael S. Barry, author of "The Forgiveness Project: The Startling Discovery of How to Overcome Cancer, Find Health and Achieve Peace" writes,

Forgiveness is a key to happiness. Forgiveness heals painful memories and creates the opportunities for the healing of relationships. Forgiveness offers "the way out". Forgiveness offers emotional, spiritual and physical healing. Forgiveness has an immediate, wholesome effect and long-term benefit. The stress of unforgiveness effects the immune system, as the ammunition that our bodies use to combat disease begins to run out.

"The payoff is nothing short of personal peace – with others, ourselves, and possibly even with God. Its benefits are priceless."[64]

As I moved through this decision to forgive, the status of my health changed. An appointment with my cardiologist a year later resulted in an improved condition. He lowered my status from "Stage A heart failure" to "a severe heart valve problem". Another year later resulted in another downgrade to "a mild heart valve problem".

God fixed my broken heart.

---

64 Michael S. Barry The Forgiveness Project: The Startling Discovery of How to Overcome Cancer, Find Health and Achieve Peace (Grand Rapids, Michigan: Kregel Publications, 2011), 79-80.

Epilogue

In spite of all I have been through, I still believe in "happily ever after". Around the same time that I left Philip, Jim strolled back into my life after a 25 year absence. We attended our 30th high school reunion together. We spent the next four years getting to know one another again and reminiscing shared history. In the beginning, we initially thought about all of the years that we had missed together. We ultimately came to the conclusion that we each needed to endure our heartbreaks and bad relationships to help us to grow and appreciate what could be. We agreed that if we had stayed together when we were young, our immaturity would have messed it all up, in spite of the purity of our love. Instead, as adults, we share an earthly love that is deeper, more genuine and more pure than anything we could have ever imagined existed.

After four years of dating as adults, Jim stunned me with a proposal of marriage on my birthday.

Just over a year later, we were married.

Four years later, Jim still makes my heart skip a beat. Our love surpasses anything we have ever known before. This will be my "happily ever after", spent with a man that my deepest heart has loved for 43 years. Jim understands my history and my story. A story that I now feel compelled to share in an effort to make a difference. My hope and desire is that others will be strengthened, encouraged, and motivated by my story; as well as by the most recent statistics, which are alarming:

Worldwide:

- 35% of women worldwide have experienced either physical and/or sexual intimate partner violence or non-partner sexual violence, according to 2013 United Nations global review of available data.

- One out of every three women has experienced intimate partner abuse during her lifetime, according to the American Psychology Association.

United States:

- Each minute – Twenty four people are victims of intimate partner violence, according to the Centers for Disease Control and Prevention.

- Each day: Three or more women are murdered by their boyfriends or husbands on average, according to the American Psychology Association.

- Each month: The National Domestic Violence Hotline receives an average of 22,000 calls.

- Each year: Over 12 million women and men are victims of intimate partner violence, according to the Centers for Disease Control and Prevention."[65]

My heart breaks with these statistics. I was one of these numbers. God had a different plan for my

---

65 www.cnn.com

life. I ask you to join me in this fight against Domestic Violence. Do whatever you can to increase awareness; to reach out a hand to help someone who simply does not know where to turn; donate time or money to domestic violence causes and shelters; positively influence a young boy in your life; teach your children about healthy relationships. Please. Do not look the other way.

I am often asked if I would do it all over again. My response is always, "Yes." My one-word response is consistently met with astonished looks and disbelief. People simply cannot understand why I would do it all over again. I made mistakes along the way. I did not always make the best decisions. Thank goodness God's grace and mercies are always available! Thirty two years after the trauma to my jaw, I am often reminded of what I went through and survived. My jaw still radiates such pain that I need heat therapy and pain relief to endure it. The pain travels up my neck and into my jaw and ear. Sometimes I am in tears because the pain is so bad. I reflect on how I tried to be a good parent. Without that magical parenting book that every parent wishes for, I did the best I could with the skills I had at the time. My only regret is that my children did not have strong male role models to look up to and emulate. Yet, in spite of it all, I would go through it again, and here are my reasons why:

- First and foremost, my children. My first marriage gave me two wonderful sons. I am so very proud of the obstacles they have overcome, their intelligence, and the men they have grown up to be. My second marriage gave me two beautiful daughters. I am so very proud of their strength and intelligence, as well as their inner and outer beauty. My second marriage also gave me an amazing stepson, who has chosen to keep me involved in his life long after my marriage to his father has ended. I am honored. My children are my greatest accomplishment in my life. Their very existence has brought me inexpressible joy and blessing beyond measure. If I had not chosen to marry their fathers, none of them would be here. My life and this planet would be less rich.

- My strength. At times when I felt that I could not take another step, an undefeatable strength rose from deep within me, and pushed me forward. Because of that strength, I know that I can endure absolutely anything that comes my way.

- My faith. I knew I had been raised with a deeply rooted faith in God, but the experiences I have had drew me closer to the personal, loving God that I know today. I have experienced His hand of protection and guidance, His abundant blessing in my life, and a profound love that words cannot express. This amazing God touches my heart in a way that no one can and draws me to tear-filled worship in peace and gratitude. He has proven to me time and time again that He keeps His promises. I am living proof of Romans 8:28. God has taken all of the bad things in my life, all of the storms, all of the pain and deepest hurts and ignited a passion within my heart to help other women who are walking the same road that I did. I am hopeful that sharing my story will help others who are being abused or have been abused. God sees what you are going through and He will use it for good. I can promise you that because God promises that. My God will not make a promise that He will not keep.

- Lastly, though certainly not least, my marriage to Jim. My previous marriages were clear displays of what marriage should not be. My marriage to Jim is a true partnership and we share an unspoken "knowing" of our love. He accepts me, respects me, encourages and supports all that I am. He can make me laugh like no one else ever has. He truly is the love of my life here on earth and I am deeply blessed to be his wife.

God could have chosen a different plan for me. I am deeply grateful to wake up each day. With His help, I fought the strongholds in my life and allowed Him to become a stronghold for me.

God had a purpose in mind when He created each of us. We need to be mindful of that as we journey through this life. *You* can make a difference. If you know someone who is being abused, do something about it. If you are being abused, ask God to provide the way to safety. He will do it. He may provide appropriate circumstances for your escape or surround you with people who can help you. I know how broken and helpless you feel. Even more, *God* knows how broken and helpless you feel.

God wants to have first place in your life. You can come to Him in all your brokenness and give Him your heart. The best thing is that God will meet you where you are. Right now. With an open heart, ask God to forgive your sins and ask Him to come into your heart. After that, take the steps necessary to honor Him with your life. Read His Word, the Bible. Get to know this Jesus. Seek fellowship in a Bible believing church. He will meet your every need and provide for you in ways that you cannot begin to imagine. He promises to give us exceedingly and abundantly more than we could ever ask or imagine. We need to ask. Wait for it! He promises and He will do it! Let God break the stronghold of abuse in your life and let Him be your stronghold as you move towards a new and amazing life.

There is something that I want you to remember. A wonderful reminder of some of God's promises to us, written by Elizabeth George in her book, "Loving God With All Your Mind", she pens as "A Note About Nothings":

Nothing will ever happen to you that God does not already know about (Psalm 139:1-4)

Nothing will ever happen to you that is a mistake (Psalm 139:4,16)

Nothing will ever happen that you cannot handle by God's power and grace (2 Corinthians 12:9,10)

Nothing will ever happen to you that will not eventually be used by God for some good purpose in your life (Romans 8:28)

Nothing will ever happen to you without God's presence (Matthew 28:20)[66]

---

66 Elizabeth George Loving God With All Your Mind (Eugene, Oregon: Harvest House Publishers, 1994/2005), 52. Used by Permission.

You were made for so much more than living a life of abuse. Wishing you courage to make changes, safety on your journey, many blessings, and an abundant life!

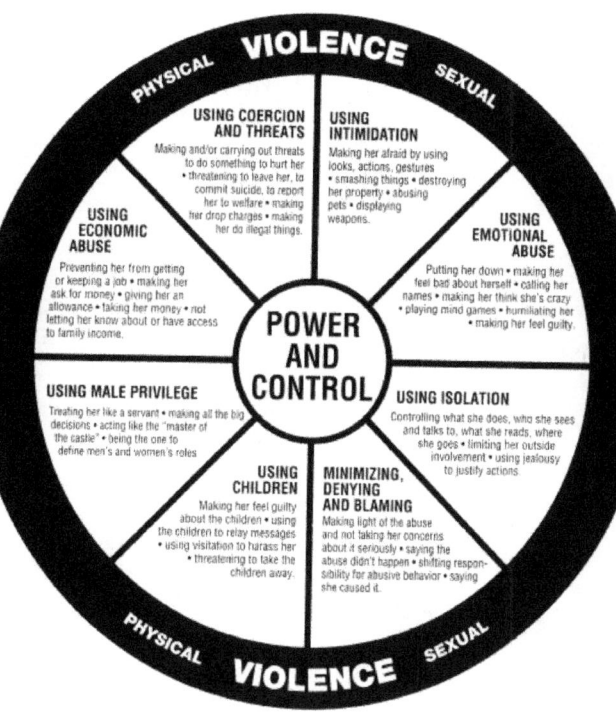

United States Domestic Violence Websites and Contact Information

If you are in immediate danger, call 9-1-1.

Help is available 24 hours a day, 7 days a week. The National Domestic Violence Hotline is 1-800-799-SAFE (7233)

I encourage you to access your state website. There is a wealth of information available to assist you with understanding Domestic Violence, as well as information to assist you if you are a victim. Every state website also has an immediate "escape" button in case of danger.

- ALASKA: Alaska Network on Domestic Violence and Sexual Assault

  www.andvsa.org

  National Domestic Violence Hotline
  1-800-799-SAFE (7233)

- ARIZONA: Arizona Coalition Against Domestic Violence

  www.azcadv.org

  602-279-2900 or 1-800-782-6400 (Monday-Friday, 8:30 am- 5:00 pm) OR

National Domestic Violence Hotline
1-800-799-SAFE (7233)

- ARKANSAS: Arkansas Coalition Against Domestic Violence

  www.domesticpeace.com

  1-800-269-4668 or 501-907-5612 during regular business hours OR

  The website contains local hotline numbers to call OR National Domestic Violence Hotline 1-800-799-SAFE (7233)

- CALIFORNIA: California Partnership to End Domestic Violence

  www.cpedv.org

  1-800-524-4765 during regular business hours OR National Domestic Violence Hotline 1-800-799-SAFE (7233)

- COLORADO: Colorado Coalition Against Domestic Violence

  www.ccadvorg

  303-831-9632 or 1-888-778-7091 during regular business hours OR

  National Domestic Violence Hotline
  1-800-799-SAFE (7233)

- CONNECTICUT: Connecticut Coalition Against Domestic Violence

    www.ctcadv.org

    Connecticut Statewide Hotline
    1-888-774-2900

- DELAWARE: Delaware Coalition Against Domestic Violence

    www.dcadv.org

    Northern Delaware 24 hr Hotline
    302-762-6110

    Southern Delaware 24 hr Hotline
    302-422-8058 OR 302-745-9874

- FLORIDA: Florida Coalition Against Domestic Violence

    www.fcadv.org

    Florida Domestic Violence Hotline
    1-800-500-1119

- GEORGIA: Georgia Coalition Against Domestic Violence

    www.gcadv.org

    Georgia Statewide Hotline 1-800-33-HAVEN (1-800-334-2836)

- HAWAII: Hawaii State Coalition Against Domestic Violence

    www.hscadv.org

    24 hr Shelter Hotlines:

    > Hilo 959-8864
    >
    > Kauai 245-6362
    >
    > Kona 322-SAFE (7233)
    >
    > Maui/Lanai 579-9581
    >
    > Molokai 567-6888
    >
    > Oahu 841-0822 (Town/Leeward)
    > 526-2200 OR 528-0606 (Windward)

- IDAHO: Idaho Coalition Against Sexual and Domestic Violence

    www.idvsa.org

    208-384-0419 during regular business hours OR National Domestic Violence Hotline 1-800-799-SAFE (7233)

- ILLINOIS: Illinois Coalition Against Domestic Violence

    www.ilcadv.org

Illinois Domestic Violence Helpline 1-877-863-6338

- INDIANA: Indiana Coalition Against Domestic Violence

  www.icadvinc.org

  Indiana Statewide Hotline 1-800-332-7385

- IOWA: Iowa Coalition Against Domestic Violence

  www.icadv.org

  Iowa Statewide Domestic Violence Hotline 1-800-942-0333

- KANSAS: Kansas Coalition Against Sexual and Domestic Violence

  www.kcsdv.org

  Kansas Crisis Hotline 1-888-END-ABUSE (1-888-363-2287)

- KENTUCKY: Kentucky Domestic Violence Association

  www.kdva.org

  Kentucky Domestic Violence Association 502-209-KDVA (5382)

- LOUISIANA: Louisiana Coalition Against Domestic Violence

  www.lcadv.org

  Louisiana Statewide Hotline 1-888-411-1333

- MAINE: Maine Coalition to End Domestic Violence

  www.mcedv.org

  Maine Statewide Domestic Violence Helpline 1-866-83-4HELP

- MARYLAND: Maryland Network Against Domestic Violence

  www.mnadv.org

  Maryland Statewide Helpline 1-800-MD-HELPS

- MASSACHUSETTS: Massachusetts Coalition Against Sexual Assault and Domestic Violence

  www.janedoe.org

  Massachusetts Safelink 1-877-785-2020

- MICHIGAN: Michigan Coalition to End Domestic and Sexual Violence

  www.mcedsv.org

National Domestic Violence Hotline
1-800-799-SAFE (7233)

- MINNESOTA: Minnesota Coalition for Battered Women

    www.mcbw.org

    Minnesota Domestic Violence Crisis Line
    1-866-223-1111

- MISSISSIPPI: Mississippi Coalition Against Domestic Violence

    www.mcadv.org

    Mississippi Statewide Hotline
    1-800-898-3234

- MISSOURI: Missouri Coalition Against Domestic and Sexual Violence

    www.mocadsv.org

    National Domestic Violence Hotline
    1-800-799-SAFE (7233)

- MONTANA: Montana Coalition Against Domestic and Sexual Violence

    www.mcadsv.com

    National Domestic Violence Hotline
    1-800-799-SAFE (7233)

- NEBRASKA: Nebraska Domestic Violence and Sexual Assault Coalition

    www.ndvsac.org

    National Domestic Violence Hotline
    1-800-799-SAFE (7233)

- NEVADA: Nevada Network Against Domestic Violence

    www.nnadv.org

    National Domestic Violence Hotline
    1-800-799-SAFE (7233)

- NEW HAMPSHIRE: New Hampshire Coalition Against Domestic and Sexual Violence

    www.nhcadsv.org

    New Hampshire Domestic Violence Hotline
    1-866-644-3574

- NEW JERSEY: New Jersey Coalition for Battered Women

    www.njcbw.org

    New Jersey Domestic Violence Hotline
    1-800-572-SAFE (7233)

- NEW MEXICO: New Mexico Coalition Against Domestic Violence

  www.nmcadv.org

  National Domestic Violence Hotline
  1-800-799-SAFE (7233)

- NEW YORK: New York State Office for the Prevention of Domestic Violence

  www.opdv.ny.gov

  New York Statewide Domestic Violence Hotline 1-800-942-6906

- PENNSYLVANIA: Pennsylvania Coalition Against Domestic Violence

  www.pcadv.org

  National Domestic Violence Hotline
  1-800-799-SAFE (7233)

- RHODE ISLAND: Rhode Island Coalition Against Domestic Violence

  www.ricadv.org

  Rhode Island Statewide Domestic Violence Helpline 1-800-494-8100

- SOUTH CAROLINA: South Carolina Coalition Against Domestic Violence and Sexual Assault

  www.sccavasa.org

  1-803-256-2900 during regular business hours OR National Domestic Violence Hotline 1-800-799-SAFE (7233)

- SOUTH DAKOTA: South Dakota Coalition Ending Domestic and Sexual Violence

  www.sdcedsv.org

  National Domestic Violence Hotline 1-800-799-SAFE (7233)

- TENNESSEE: Tennessee Coalition to End Domestic and Sexual Violence

  www.tncoalition.org

  Tennessee Statewide Domestic Violence Hotline 1-800-356-6767

- TEXAS: Texas Council on Family Violence

  www.tcfv.org

  National Domestic Violence Hotline 1-800-799-SAFE (7233)

- UTAH: Utah Domestic Violence Coalition

www.udvs.org

Utah Statewide Domestic Violence Linkline 1-800-897-LINK (5465)

- VERMONT: Vermont Network Against Domestic and Sexual Violence

www.vtnetwork.org

Vermont Statewide Domestic Violence Hotline 1-800-228-7395

- VIRGINIA: Virginia Sexual and Domestic Violence Action Alliance

www.vsdvalliance.org

Virginia Family Violence and Sexual Assault Hotline 1-800-838-8238

- WASHINGTON, D.C.: District of Columbia Coalition Against Domestic Violence

www.dccadv.org

My Sister's Place 202-529-5991

DC Rape Crisis Center Hotline 1-800-656-HOPE (4673)

- WASHINGTON: Washington State Coalition Against Domestic Violence

www.wscadv2.org

Washington State Domestic Violence Hotline
1-800-562-6025

- WEST VIRGINIA: West Virginia Coalition Against Domestic Violence

   www.wvcadv.org

   National Domestic Violence Hotline
   1-800-799-SAFE (7233)

- WISCONSIN: Wisconsin Coalition Against Domestic Violence

   www.endabusewi.org

   National Domestic Violence Hotline
   1-800-799-SAFE (7233)

- WYOMING: Wyoming Coalition Against Domestic Violence

   www.wyomingdvsa.org

   Wyoming Coalition Hotline 1-800-990-3877